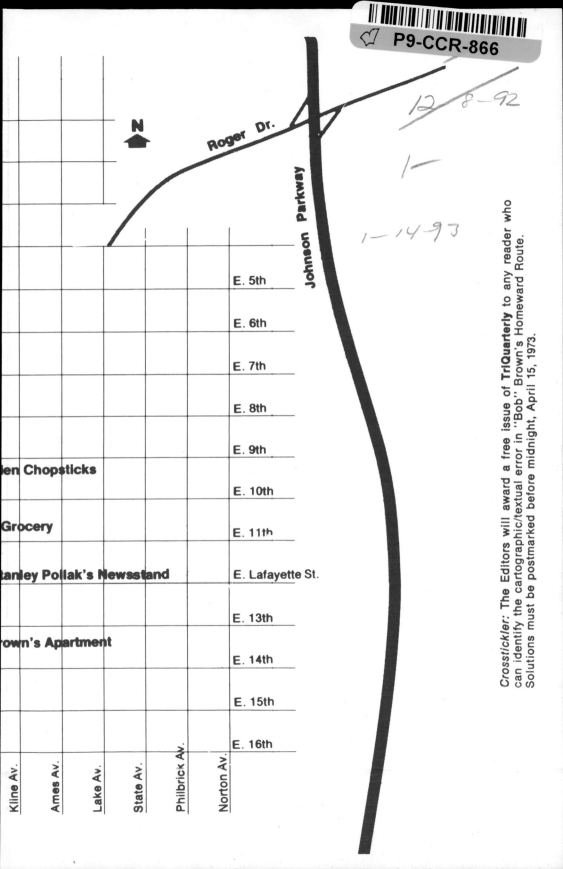

N

Roger Dr.

Johnson Parkway

12/8-92

1-14 93

E. 5th

E. 6th

E. 7th

E. 8th

E. 9th

en Chopsticks

E. 10th

Grocery

E. 11th

tanley Pollak's Newsstand

E. Lafayette St.

E. 13th

own's Apartment

E. 14th

E. 15th

E. 16th

Kline Av.

Ames Av.

Lake Av.

State Av.

Philbrick Av.

Norton Av.

Crosstickler: The Editors will award a free issue of **TriQuarterly** to any reader who can identify the cartographic/textual error in "Bob" Brown's Homeward Route. Solutions must be postmarked before midnight, April 15, 1973.

Parodies, Etcetera & So Forth

W.B. Scott

Edited by Gerald Graff and Barbara Heldt

Preface by Gerald Graff

Northwestern University Press

Published 1985 by Northwestern University Press, Evanston, Illinois. All rights reserved. Originally entitled *Chicago Letter and Other Parodies* published in 1978 by Ardis, Ann Arbor, Michigan.

ISBN 0-8101-0673-6 (cloth) 0-8101-0674-4 (paper)

Acknowledgements:
"Letter for a Festschrift" and "A 'Bob' Brown Sampler" reprinted by permission of *TriQuarterly*. "An interview with Ed Rasmussen," "Clutter Counters Everywhere," "*Furioso's* Nosegay of Critics,"
"$_7N^{15} + _1H^1 + _6C^{12} + _2He^4$" and "Chicago Letter" reprinted by permission of *Furioso*.

CONTENTS

for Lizzie

Preface

In a letter of May 9, 1950, Edmund Wilson wrote to Vladimir Nabokov ("Dear Volodya") that he was enclosing "another *Furioso*, with another burlesque by Scott. His French is no good, but the parody of Gide I thought very funny—it sounds just like the last installment of his diary. Zane Grey was a writer of romantic Westerns, of whom you may never have heard." Nabokov, replying on May 15, agreed with Wilson on the merits of the piece but disagreed (as he and Wilson were wont to do on linguistic matters) on the French. Nabokov wrote that "Scott's piece is admirable. His French seemed to me quite good though Véra says she detected a few wrong tenses—but then Frenchmen make mistakes too. The whole thing is very funny and successful." The exchange appears in *The Nabokov-Wilson Letters, 1940–1971*, edited by Simon Karlinsky (New York, 1979). The "burlesque" in question was entitled "Gaëtan Fignole: Pages de Journal," and the "Scott" was Walter B. Scott, Jr., a professor of theatre whose satiric writings were appearing frequently in the pages of *Furioso* in the late forties and early fifties.

In his fine collection, *Parodies: an Anthology from Chaucer to Beerbohm—and After* (1960), Dwight Macdonald described *Furioso*, under the editorship of Reed Whittemore from 1946 to 1953 (later revived by Whittemore as *The Carleton Miscellany*), as a magazine "distinguished for humor and irreverence." Macdonald reprinted "Gaëtan Fignole" and another *Furioso* piece, "Chicago Letter," and in his prefatory note said publicly what "Volodya" and "Bunny" had expressed privately:

> . . . one of *Furioso's* happiest discoveries was the parodic talent of Walter B. Scott, who teaches dramatic literature at Northwestern University. His *Chicago Letter* below is a cry from the heart against the more precious and insider-oriented snobberies of our Little Magazines; I think he must have had some of *Partisan Review's* foreign correspondents in mind. As for Mr. Scott's other contribution ["Gaëtan Fignole"], those who have suffered from an even more precious and cliquest quality in certain memoirs of certain recent French writers will have no trouble identifying the originals of Mr. Fignole and his journal.

What Macdonald called "the more precious and insider-oriented snobberies of our Little Magazines" is a frequent target of Scott's best satire. Here, for example, are the suitably tremulous opening paragraphs of "Chicago Letter":

> Agony, a sense of plight; a sense of agony, plight—such, one soon perceives, are the attributes of the Chicago of our time. But I shall have more to say about them later in this letter.
> I travelled by the Erie, as one must, I think, do, now and then. The trip is longer, to be sure, on its ancient twisting right-of-way than on other roads. But there one escapes the *"lumpen-aristokratie"* (in Roscoe Chutney's phrase) of the Century or the Broadway, and it is only from the Erie, of course, that one may catch those extraordinary night glimpses of Youngstown and Akron.

Of course, of course. . . . A number of things make this passage sail parodically, but for me it is the placement of "I think," "to be sure," and "of course" that creates that effect of agonizingly hard-earned hyperscrupulousness (I think) that the kind of intellectual being parodied (to be sure) likes to think he is achieving (of course).

I'm tempted to go on quoting from "Chicago Letter" here, but I would soon have quoted the whole thing, which you can better read in this collection—along with "Gaëtan Fignole" and other pieces from *Furioso* and the *Carleton Miscellany* not heretofore reprinted. These include "Clutter Counters Everywhere," "*Furioso's* Nosegay of Critics," "Interview With Ed Rasmussen," and "$_7N^{15} + {}_1H^1 + {}_6C^{12} + {}_2He^4$," more familiarly known as the Carbon Cycle. Written three decades ago, these pieces are as fresh and pertinent as ever.

When I joined the faculty of Northwestern University in 1966, I was naturally eager to meet the man who had written these hilarious works. What I didn't know and was soon to my delight to find out was that only a fraction of Walter Scott's best satiric writing had been written for publication. Aided by the Northwestern Theatre Department's hardworking mimeograph machine (in the lost days before the xerox revolution), Walter ran a one-man office industry which produced an unendingly delightful, not infrequently outrageous, stream of letters, parodies, travesties, faked official notices, faked photographs, and other items falling under no known classification. Many of these creations were wildly (at times obscenely) illustrated with cut-outs from newspapers and magazines or drawings from Walter's own hand, for Walter had the gift of translating his writer's sense of the whimsical into line drawings. The illustrations in this book (including those on the dustjacket) are Scott's.

The products of the Scott workshop went out almost daily to Northwestern colleagues, administrators, and students lucky enough to be on Walter's mailing-list. Walter had come to Northwestern (after his Ph.D. from Princeton) in 1939, and colleagues of long standing like Harrison Hayford, J. Lyndon Shanley, Richard Ellmann, Wallace Douglas, Carl Condit, Ruth Marcus, and George Cohen had been receiving his work—and often appearing in it—for many years. At the period when I arrived, many of Walter's parody-ideas were being hatched in the conversations at our roundtable lunches at Michelini's Restaurant in Evanston. Walter's productions continued after his retirement from Northwestern in 1978, punctuated by occasional publications in Northwestern's *TriQuarterly.* They ceased only with his death, at the age of 72, in March, 1980.

As one would expect, much of Scott's privately-circulated material is of too occasional or intramural a nature to interest general readers. But after sifting, numerous pieces remain which compare favorably in general appeal with Scott's published work. In 1977, Barbara Heldt and I, with Scott's consent and assistance, made a selection of published and unpublished writings, which was published in 1978 by Ardis of Ann Arbor under the title, *Chicago Letter and Other Parodies.* Ardis is a small publisher primarily noted for its list in Russian literature and criticism, not for books of satire and parody. *Chicago Letter* received, so far as I know, only one review, that one appearing locally in *Chicago Magazine* (written by Jonathan Brent, now Associate Director and Editor of Northwestern University Press). I know that many readers who have come to love the book did not become aware of its existence until long after its publication, either stumbling on it eventually by accident or hearing about it through a friend. It seems likely that many potential fans are still unaware of its existence. Which explains the reason for this reprint (under a new title with new illustrations and a new editorial preface), through which we hope to bring W. B. Scott's superb satire to a wider readership. For the origins of the title phrase, "etcetera and so forth," see below, pp. 26–27.

Like the best literary parodies, those of Scott achieve a fine balance between sympathetic mimicry and critical distance, admiration and irony. Really good parody springs from an intimacy with its subjects which can't be faked but has to come from living for years in the presence of the author. It also has to have an edge to it. A case in point illustrating both qualities is Scott's parody of "The Cocktail Party," which, for my money anyway, is a better piece of work than T. S. Eliot's play and is unquestionably more fun to read:

Yes.
I have seen Mildred. I saw her at the station
And drove out with her. She will be here shortly,
As soon as she has paid the taxi driver
And brought her luggage up to the house.
You must ask me no more questions. And you must
Promise that you will not ask *Mildred* any questions.

REGINALD [Mildred's husband]

But that makes me feel like an utter fool, Ogden.
Why should I not ask Mildred any questions?

OGDEN

Because you *are* an utter fool, Reginald.
And because you have never faced up
To the Reginald whom you thought you saw this morning
Offering his chin to your razor in the mirror.
You must find the answer to this yourself.
I can only show that there may *be* an answer.

"The Reginald whom you thought you saw this morning/Offering his chin to your razor in the mirror" is both splendidly Eliotic and idiotic—very close to Eliot's actual manner but just pretentiously inflated enough to make its point. But again I must resist the temptation to go on quoting and marvelling so you can get to the full, unmediated W. B. Scott, "W. B. Scott in the raw," as Richard Ellmann says. Let me end by saying that writing like this is not only literary criticism of the most acute kind, but literature in its own right, whatever you take "literature" to be. A Great Tradition of Parody would probably be a contradiction in terms, the aim of parody being to make one think twice about speaking of great traditions. But if there were such a tradition, W. B. Scott would be in it.

* * * * *

Scott's pieces occasionally contain "inside" references to local persons, places, and events, while others refer to contexts or writings no longer current. These references will pose no serious problem for readers, but a brief word here about a few of them may be helpful.

"The Problem of Tragedy" was inspired by a letter written by the great University of Chicago critic, Ronald S. Crane, in response to a former student's interpretations of Hemingway's story, "The Short Happy Life of Francis Macomber." Crane's letter was published in 1949 in the *English A Analyst,* a mimeographed journal then produced by the

Northwestern English Department, and was reprinted, with modifications, in Crane's *The Idea of the Humanities and Other Essays Critical and Historical,* edited by Wayne Booth (Chicago, 1967), vol. 2.

"Canto 101" and "Mosher, Prince of Swabia" refer to local faculty activities as well as to Pound and Shakespeare.

"Notes on the Early History of the Term 'Jazz'" was mimeographed and distributed at a public concert given by a faculty jazz group. Many Jazz afficionados were taken in.

"Vis'ting Fireman" gives some idea what Ben Jonson might have thought about certain eminent visiting professors of literature.

"A Minor Elizabethan was first sprung on unsuspecting Northwestern undergraduates as part of their final examination in a course in English Drama of the Renaissance. Students were asked to comment on those aspects of the life and writing of "Christopher 'Kit' Pilchard" which made him so seemingly typical of the dramatists of the Renaissance—aspects Scott saw to it were abundantly provided in the excerpts from Pilchard's verse tragedy and the purported account by the noted Renaissance scholar, Professor Giovanni Cavallo.

Cinéma whips the traditional French literary interview into definitive shape.

"Letter for a Festschrift" appeared among the tributes to Nabokov collected in *Vladimir Nabokov on his Seventieth Birthday,* edited by Alfred Appel, Jr. and Charles Newman and published as *TriQuarterly,* 17 (Winter, 1970), reprinted by Northwestern University Press (1970). Commenting on the Feschrift in a *New York Times* interview (March 18, 1970), Nabokov singled out Scott's Pnin-esque "Letter" as "a masterpiece. It was so full of plums," he added, "that I read it three times. It's absolutely splendid."

"A 'Bob' Brown Sampler," written in collaboration with me, appeared in *TriQuarterly,* 26 (Winter 1973). The map of "'Bob' Brown's homeward route" and the accompanying contest announcement were not included in the Ardis edition. Something like seven or eight readers identified the errors (more than intended) and were duly rewarded.

Gerald Graff
March, 1985

Parodies, Etcetera & So Forth

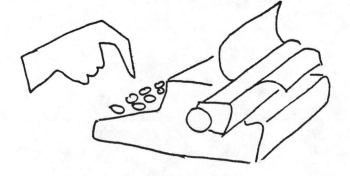

Chicago Letter

April, 1949

"Voyage infortuné! Rivage malheureux,
Falloit-il approcher de tes bords dangereux?"
—Racine

Agony, a sense of plight; a sense of agony, plight—such, one soon perceives, are the attributes of the Chicago of our time. But I shall have more to say about them later in this letter.

I travelled by·the Erie, as one must, I think, do, now and then. The trip is longer, to be sure, on its ancient twisting right-of-way than on other roads. But there one escapes the *"lumpen-aristokratie"* (in Roscoe Chutney's phrase) of the Century or the Broadway, and it is only from the Erie, of course, that one may catch those extraordinary night glimpses of Youngstown and Akron.

I had not planned to do much reading on the train, but re-calling how trying the journey could be (in certain weathers) between Hankins and Horseheads, I had as a precaution bought the latest *Peristalsis* at a kiosk in the Jersey City station. It was thus, at lunch (in the diner) that I happened upon Hjalmar Ekdal's essay, "Kafka's Ulcer"—a subject I had outlined to Hjalmar at Ocean Grove in the late summer of 1945. Had he quite *realized* it, though, in Cézanne's sense? I could not, at the moment, be entirely certain.

Some hours later, settled in my berth (there is something to be said for the old standard sleeper, after all), and glancing through the rest of the magazine (which [as it happened] I had no clear intention of reading then), I discovered Mildred's Bel-grade Letter, Sam's Naples Letter, Boris's Pskov Letter, Fred's Capetown Letter, Deirdre's Quito Letter, Jaroslav's Paris Letter, and Harry's Prague Letter. These were precisely the people I had looked forward most to seeing in Chicago, and it was small comfort to be told (on my arrival) of the fate already suffered by several of them—Boris and Harry shot by Stalinists (on a

3

trumped-up charge of cosmopolitan rootlessness), Mildred hanged by Titoists in the woods north of Slunj, Sam abducted by the resurgent Mafia, Deirdre raped, robbed, and butchered by Clerical-Trotskyists. How explain these horrors? Those who remained in Chicago shrugged their shoulders in anxious silence at my question. What was in store for others, who had just left or were about to leave—Erma and Roscoe Chutney, already on their way to Shiraz; the Ekdals, who were departing the day after my arrival?

"It doesn't much matter where I go," Hjalmar told me. "Hatred and envy are my shadows. I had thought of the Yukon, God knows why, but Gina's already promised two Aleppo Letters to *Peristalsis,* so I suppose we might as well go there. Is it true that they still use the old water torture in Aleppo? One might (at least) have that to look forward to."

I could not tell him: I have not been in Aleppo since I was eight or nine. All the same, I knew that Hjalmar was suffering. Kafka's ulcer had, in some sense, become *his* ulcer. Or, was the world his ulcer? Does our proper pleasure in Kafka lie (after all) in this mutual *anagnorisis* of symptoms—in what I have ventured elsewhere[1] to describe as "an act of critical nosology"?

I had not yet become aware of Hjalmar's torment when Jens Kobold met me at Dearborn Station—where the grimy Victorian interior has been entirely remodelled (I do not allude, of course, to the trainshed, but to the waiting-rooms, ticket-counters, and so on) in what may best be called a sort of middle-upperbrow notion of "modern" *décor.* As for Jens, he seemed during the first few seconds much as ever—monolithic, *rébarbatif,* with that quality of tempered urgency which Roscoe Chutney has so profoundly pictured in *The Critical Stud-Book.* But as we drove through the rotting streets of the Loop and the Near North Side, I detected something new: he appeared discrete, shattered. His only reply to my questions was to spit from the taxi window and mumble an evasive phrase about riots in

---

1. "Criticism as Diagnosis." *Peristalsis,* Winter-Summer, 1943.

4

the Bosnian quarter. I could not imagine what he meant: there is always rioting in Chicago's Bosnian quarter, and Jens had always boasted his entire indifference to *la question bosnienne*. For the moment I said no more, and contemplated the buildings and the hoardings. On one of these latter, an enormous photomural (of Truman Capote [I think] balanced perilously in ballet costume on a high wire) had already been savagely ripped by the lake wind. But worse was to come.

At Jens's studio pretty much all that was left of the *premier rang* of Chicago's *avant garde* was spiritlessly waiting for us: the Ekdals, appalled by the amount of packing still to be done and by the strawberry rash which Gina's ringworm shots had produced; Bernard Mosher, apprehensively drunk; George Barnwell, Maire Ni Laoghaire, Jeremy Irk (unshakeably gloomy, despite the putative success of his new play—of which more later).

The party was, of course, a desperate failure: I find it a torture to record my own corrosive memories of it. The lovely Maire no longer stretched on the floor with Jeremy to say wise dreadful things about Dostoevsky; now she sat hunched and nearly silent on the Grand Rapids divan which is so familiar and amusing a shape in Jens's pictures of the '30's. As for the others—but why persist on this level of discourse? I sensed that much was missing—but what? Recently I had read somewhere that French intellectuals are gayer, less elegiac than their opposite numbers in America. I had not dreamed, however, that American intellectuals are so little gay, so formidably elegiac. What was the nexus?

In the course of that long, disenchanted first day in Chicago I discovered that Jens had given up easel painting, and that he now, in his phrase, "soils" pages torn at random from the *Tribune,* at which he flings wildly-punctured cans of ten-cent-store oil paint. The results are, of course, often magnificent—Maire Ni Laoghaire has written superbly of Jen's *jetage*—but all the same they hint (possibly) at something not far removed from uncertainty—an uncertainty even more apparent in the work of those imitators of his who have attempted the same sort of thing with the *Sun-Times* or *Herald-American.* I cannot avoid being enormously impressed by many of these new pictures of Jens's, yet I find it not easy to conceive what is central to their strategy. Jens himself, who once talked and wrote so copiously about the nature of life and painting, labels them—almost hatefully—as "Tribunemalerei," and appears contemptuous of the opinions of Maire, with whom (I am told) he is no longer living.

It was Bernard Mosher who first found precise words for what I had sensed of menace and despair in Chicago. "Call it what you will," he said as we walked along Van Buren street after seeing the Ekdals off, "it is, in my phrase, 'a sense of plight.' " At this point he left me abruptly (we had reached the corner of Van Buren and Wells), and I turned north in the shadow of the "L" for my first stroll in the doomed city.

A casual visitor might not at first glance suspect the tragic tension which torments Chicago's intellectuals and artists. Trifles are taken for wonders: under the administration of Mayor Kennelly political corruption has ceased, and what the philistine press calls "vice" has been driven out (I have yet to meet a police reporter who truly apprehends the nature of original sin). Lake Michigan seems, on the surface, unchanged. The same dingy pigeons swarm for peanuts on the "L" platforms of the Loop, and the shabby skyscrapers blot out the afternoon sun. The new streetcars already look old (as everything new looks old in Chicago). Towards the end of the day they are filled, in monotonous ritual fashion, with anthropoid businessmen frowning heavily over the *Daily News,* and bored high-school girls carelessly swinging their eternal battered copies of *The Brothers Karamazov.* On Sundays humorless bourgeois families go picnicking in the fogs along the Drainage Canal, or watch the passionless "play" of the White Sox or the Cubs (also gripped by plight—of [I suspect] a rather different order).

Little by little, as the leaden hours slog by in this joyless metropolis, one clutches at further tokens of the truth of

6

Bernard Mosher's *aperçu.* I do not (of course) propose to burden this letter with statistics, but where are the great Chicago essays of the mid-1940's?[2] Who, for example, writes about Melville now? Three years ago the mean annual production in Cook County of Melville books and articles was 274; today it is scarcely fifteen. Three years ago we were finding new hope in George Barnwell's "Melville's Whale and M. de Charlus," Hjalmar Ekdal's "Melville's Tumor," Bernard Mosher's "Barnwell, Ekdal, and the Melville World." Nowadays one encounters, at best—and it is simply not good enough—some Northwestern University pedant's cynical and barren, "Smile When You Call Me Ishmael." Und weiter nichts.

Other facts suggest the city's agony. A fortnight after my arrival I read in the *Cicero Quarterly* (which last week ceased publication) of the dissolution of the Goose Island Sartre Club, whose president, with ironic ambivalence, rather than commit suicide had taken a job as check-out boy in a supermarket. Early today, as I started to compose this letter, Jeremy Irk phoned to tell me that the Rogers Park *Cercle Rimbaud* is down to nine members, eight of whom do not speak to each other. Yet, with all this endemic apathy, one learns of eruptions of violence as well (I do not here allude to the Bosnian riots, of course). In the dim alleys of the South Side, I am told, "goon squads" from the Aristotle A. C. sally out after nightfall to sack hostile bookshops or worse. Such things are, to be sure, a kind of action, although I cannot say what hope one is to take from it.

It is along South State and North Clark streets that one is most sharply conscious of the pervasive sense of plight. Here, as in the past, one discovers the youth of the *avant garde,* but now much altered—frustrated painters, *poètes par trop manqués,* defeated composers, disappointed novelists, exhausted sculptors, beaten playwrights, embittered critics, bilious critics of critics, all of them shivering in the cold spring rain, but too

2. One recalls, above all, perhaps, Irk and Chutney, "The Heresy of Fallacy" *(Peristalsis,* Winter-Summer, 1945); Chutney and Irk, "The Fallacy of Heresy" *(Peristalsis,* Winter-Summer, 1946).

tired, indolent, indifferent to seek the relative warmth of the bars. I do not propose to intrude upon my readers that improbable figure of American myth, the philosophical bartender, but I did chance upon one old man—he had known Kierkegaard at Trondhjem, as it happened—who put the case for me about as clearly as anyone else had done. I was watching him construct North Clark street's favorite drink, a double *pousse-café,* and as he worked at it with his precise artist's fingers, he nodded through the door towards the crowds outside.

"These kids got the sense of plight so bad they ain't even writing or talking about it, nor trying to reduce it somehow to canvas or stone," he said. "You take as recent as six, eight months ago they'd r'ar up and snap at each other like they was Stanley Edgar Kazin. You know how I mean—'Jake that dope he don't really unnerstand the nature of Myth,' 'Mike, all the psychoanalysis he ever read, *if* he ever read it, is Joseph Jastrow,' 'Moe combines ignorance wit brashness to an amazing degree,' 'Joe's got about as much innerest in the *text* of a poem—by which I mean *what* a poem *is*—as a Van Buren street pigeon has in clean feathers.' In there pitching. This joint used to sound like it was, you might say, collective criticism by symposium going on all the time. But what do they do now? Just set out there in the rain on the *terrasse* and mope. I ain't even heard Hemingway sneered at in rising two months. You looking for the sense of plight, boy, you come to the right town!"

If plight has come close to silencing the artists and critics, it has (for all practical purposes) obliterated the philosophers and political theorists. A few, I gather, have entered general semantics, a few have killed themselves or each other. As for still others—

"Tout fuit; et sans s'armer d'un courage inutile,
Dans le temple voisin chacun cherche un asile"

in Racine's sense of the phrase. Only yesterday the Café Désespoir et du Terminus closed its doors. The Heidegger Bar and Grill has (I hear) taken to watering its *pousse-cafés.* Where is an answer to be found?

8

It is clearly not to be found in the Chicago theatre. In the commodity houses of the Loop one is faced (inevitably) with pure *Kitsch*—ill-made well-made plays, well-made ill-made plays, tepidly performed before drowsy lower-middle-brow audiences which wake into sudden anxious laughter at bathroom jokes, then sink back into the somnolence of the damned.

The best theatre in Chicago was available (I use "was" here in its sense of past tense of "to be") very distant from the Loop, in an abandoned warehouse on the Far Northwest Side, where one climbed four flights of condemned wooden stairs to a make-shift hall under a decaying roof. The second-hand seats in the orchestra, gnawed incessantly by rats, were scantily occupied by bewildered bourgeois couples and drunken slummers from the Gold Coast. The rickety balcony was packed with sullen students, who showed little interest in what was going on, little sign of the passion for theatre which may once have possessed them.

Maire Ni Laoghaire took me one night to see Jean-Jean Baroque act Jeremy Irk's *Les Voyeurs de Rogers Park,* in Irk's own extraordinary translation. This is (in some respects) a puzzling play, and until I have read the script, I shall not venture to pronounce a final judgment on it. "Mordant, plangent, repellent," (in Maire Ni Laoghaire's phrase) it is at once strikingly astringent, yet rather like warm marshmallows. There are eight acts (five of them, of course, in verse) of which the first three, played in a blackout, are almost hauntingly rhetorical. But more than any other play I have seen in years (in London, Paris, New York, Rome, Moscow, Stambouli, Narvik, that is), Irk's drama comes to close grips with certain deeply-imbedded constituents of the American myth—particularly various suburban *rites de passage* reminiscent—at first hearing, in any event—of those which Rudge observed in Lower Borneo. I am persuaded, however, that Irk's parallel between Salmon P. Chase and the Corn God may be at once too tenuous and too obvious.

But I shall not attempt to summarize the play here—the fourth and seventh acts are to appear in the Winter-Summer

9

Peristalsis—because I wish to comment rather on the amazing art of Baroque. An ugly little man, with a whiskey baritone which engaged one like a wood rasp (I have heard that he had been [at one time] a bouncer in the Pump Room), he was able to transmute himself into an entire world of characters, none of them conventional and all of them complex. In the course of the action he was by turns (one could almost swear simultaneously, and this may, indeed, have been in large measure the *clef* of his achievement) an existentialist high-school junior, a "bop" xylophonist, a sentimental police sergeant, a sort of philosophy professor, a myopic anthropologist, Raskolnikov's ghost, and the oldest sadist in Rogers Park. Baroque made impressively little use of his body: "He seems," Maire Ni Laoghaire told me, "somehow to do it all with his skin." Did Baroque betray the sense of plight? There was not time for me to ascertain an answer to this question.

It may, very possibly, have been a greater tragedy for the Chicago stage, and for our decomposing culture in general, than we yet realize, when (two days after my visit, as it happened) the theatre suddenly caved in, and Baroque (with his entire company), three bourgeois couples, a sodden debutante and her elderly lover, innumerable rats, and the balconyful of students were plunged four flights into a flooded basement. All of them were crushed to death, or drowned. I cannot (it seems to me) escape the conviction that this incident was a further token of the city's fate—perhaps (though, of course, by no means certainly) more momentous than most.

Jeremy Irk, staggered as he was by this occurrence, has not yet been able to complete his poem about it. But I was fortunate enough to inspect several fragments of the work in progress before they (together with Bernard Mosher's discussion of them) were shipped off to Buffalo, and I am privileged to announce that Irk's work is quite *indicible*. I had, of course, hoped to persuade Jeremy to allow their publication with this letter, but he refused with the tired, broken smile which he had learned so well from Jens Kobold's portrait of him.

"It's too late," he said, although I had pointed out to him that publication of his fragments might be one means of leading the city out of its plight.

"Too late... too late," he continued. (These words cling to one like lint in the Chicago of the mid-twentieth century.) "It is too late for too many things. Too late for Maire's film on Bernard Mosher. Too late for Gina's ballet, though the slippers have already been ordered. Too late for Erma Chutney's novel about our common predicament. It is too late for Roscoe Chutney's study of Hjalmar as critic, and for Hjalmar's monograph on Jens's lithographs. It is too late for George Barnwell to take issue with Roscoe. It is too late for Jens's note, with sketches, on Gina's choreography. It is, of course, much too late for Bernard's book on Maire. Like an arthritic juggler, one feels no longer able to keep the balls in the air. It is just too late."

I shall, perhaps, let these words of Jeremy's stand in this letter as a kind of epiphany, in the various senses of the word.

* * *

"On dit qu'un prompt départ vous éloigne de nous,
Seigneur."

—Racine

Tonight I propose to quit this crumbling city. I have just observed in the *Official Railway Guide* that the International Limited on the Grand Trunk leaves for Halifax at 8 p.m. But my copy of the *Guide* is dated November, 1944, and belongs, thus, one suspects, to another world. The time may be wrong. Perhaps this train has been cancelled. Perhaps the timetable of the Grand Trunk has achieved (at last) a fresh and more telling synthesis. Yet, if not this train, then another.

I shall not tell Maire, who has expressed a desire (which it would not [all things considered] be improper to call insistent) to go with me when I go. It might be rather amusing to show her the bleak old city on its crags, to introduce her to the *avant garde* of Nova Scotia. But I cannot risk carrying any part of Chicago with me: I take it that my Halifax Letter must concern itself with Halifax *as* Halifax.

11

Perhaps there too I shall encounter a sense of plight. Perhaps it is not limited to Chicago or to Halifax. One wonders about these things as one packs, looking out of one's window at the slatey April sky of Chicago, at the lethargic gulls sagging listlessly towards the bruise-colored lake. One wonders. But one cannot, of course, be quite sure.

1949

The Problem of Tragedy

UNIVERSITY OF GARY

The Birching Room   5 November 1949

Dear Mr. Hayford,

Thank you very much for sending me your article on the *Chicago Telephone Directory, September, 1948,* as well as the articles on this work by your associates, Douglas Minor and Shanley Minor. I cannot agree in all respects with any of these articles, although I find somewhat less to object to in yours than in the other two. For both Douglas Minor and Shanley Minor seem to be less concerned with the structure of the work itself than with imposing upon it abstract theories which have no necessary connections with it; I refer particularly to Douglas Minor's assertion that the *Directory* "reflects the racial tensions of our time in a grossly biassed way" and to Shanley Minor's announcement, in his opening sentences, that the work is "a silly piece of business" and that he "can't be bothered to read a telephone book more than two pages long." Douglas Minor has failed sufficiently to consider the long lists of Cohens, Levys, and so on, as necessary parts of the plot; Shanley Minor arbitrarily prejudges the work and has clearly ignored the question of magnitude of which Aristotle speaks early in the *Poetics.*

As for your own attempts to demonstrate that Placy F. Lagioia is the hero of the *Directory*, and that he meets Aristotle's definition of the hero of tragedy, I can't agree with you at all. You base your argument upon the fact that Mr. Lagioia appears on page 1030, just half-way through the *Directory,*—in short, in a position which you call most significant with respect to Aristotle's definition. But I can find no support in the *Poetics* for your view, but quite the contrary. For Aristotle's description of the hero involves, you may recall, a man of the middling sort, neither entirely good nor entirely wicked, who through some error of judgment or *hamartia* brings about a change from good to bad fortune which involves himself and his friends and relatives. Now I think you have confused this conception of the middling man, a moral conception, with crude notions of position. Mr. Lagioia occupies the middling position in the *Directory,* but he is not therefore and of necessity a middling sort of man in Aristotle's sense. And indeed when we come to seek further evidence to support your conclusions, we find none at all. For if we assume that the hero of tragedy must suffer a change from good to bad fortune through some sort of peripety, we must also assume that he is present throughout much of the action, which must have a beginning, a middle, and an end. Now Mr. Lagioia does not appear before the mention of his name on page 1030, nor does he ever again appear in the *Directory,* and while he may be said to have a middle, he doesn't have either a beginning or an end. Far from calling him a tragic hero, I think we must put him down simply as one of the many incidental characters with which this work of the Bell Company is somewhat overcrowded.

If we assume that the hero must be present throughout much of the action, the place to seek his first appearance is clearly not half way through the work, but towards the beginning, as in *Hamlet,* or at the beginning, as in Sophocles' *Oedipus Rex.* For it should be clear that we can't feel the proper emotion of pity for a character of whose existence we are not even aware (Mr. Lagioia), nor can we find anything to arouse fear in circumstances of which we have no knowledge. And pity and fear are the emotions towards the arousing of which (with the end a purging or *katharsis* of such emotions in ourselves) tragedy is intended.

Who then, *is* the hero of the *Chicago Telephone Directory, September, 1948*? The first name mentioned in this work is "A concrete finishing," and this is followed by "A extermination," "A radio service," "A Aababox Packaging Matrls Co," and many others of like nature. Now it is evident, I think, that none of these can be the hero, for these are the names not of persons but of business firms, and the hero of tragedy is always a person and never a business firm. The first *person* mentioned in the *Directory,* in distinction to the first business firm, is Nathan Aabel, for I think we may disregard "Aabach A Plastering Co" as being in

14

all probability the name of another business firm. Shanley Minor's assertion that "Aabach A" is the name of the plastering company's owner and hence the name of the first person simply betrays, I think, the fact that this is as far as Shanley Minor got in his rather impatient reading of the *Directory.* As for Douglas Minor's theory that there is something suspect in the kind of name that Nathan Aabel seems to be, we can put this down to his attempt, which I have already mentioned, to impose a ready-made pattern on the work rather than consider its necessary conditions.

Nathan Aabel, then, is the hero of the *Directory,* to the extent that the work may be said to have a hero. And this qualification is an important one. For what, after all, do we know about Nathan Aabel? That he is an accountant. That his address (whether business or home or both is not made clear) is 902 W. Addison. That his telephone number is Lakeview 5-8819. But beyond these facts we know nothing about him, nor do we ever learn anything more. He appears once, briefly, and is gone; certainly he is far from being a tragic hero in Aristotle's sense: there is no change from good to bad fortune; there is not even a change from bad to good fortune; there is no change at all. And if there is no change at all, then we must exclude the possibilities of pity and fear. What the Bell Company has done is cynically to reduce the character almost to a nullity: notice such elements of style as "acct" for "accountant," "LAkvw" for "Lakeview," and so on. If, then, we can't accept your theory that Placy F. Lagioia is the hero, and if Nathan Aabel manifestly isn't the hero (for while *he* has a *beginning,* he has neither a middle nor an end) who then *is* the hero? I think we must conclude that there is no hero in this work, and lacking a hero no tragedy, and lacking a tragedy no pity and fear, and lacking pity and fear none of the emotions proper to tragedy. The *Directory* is simply a collection of names, arranged according to some arbitrary alphabetical order; it is an example of that kind of plot, the Episodic, which Aristotle called the worst kind of plot, since it has neither probability nor necessity in the sequence of its episodes. How much more effective, from these points of view, are other works of the Bell Company—

the *Cleveland Directory of 1924,* for example.

As for your other questions—for example, what is gained by the inclusion of such a name as Basil R. Fudge (page 596)—I could not answer them without re-reading the *Directory,* which I have no intention of doing, for I am sick and tired of it, and almost blind as well, and moreover quite frozen by the cold draught under my desk. I suspect that the Bell Company started the work with some intention (which it would not be legitimate to mention) of dealing with the tragedy of Nathan Aabel, but soon let themselves be turned from this original purpose by thoughts of the large mixed public audience at which the *Directory* was directed.

Very cordially yours,
Donald Egret

1949

The Book

Two or perhaps three nights ago I was sitting in the tub in the bathroom of our house soaking in a hot bath and reading a book. This was a small tattered book of short stories bound in paper which I had found lying on the tank of the toilet in this bathroom of ours. One of the stories was by a man named Sherwood and I thought while I was sitting there in the tub reading this story that it was many years since I had read a story by Sherwood. Twenty, even twenty-five years ago, when I was much younger I used to read many of Sherwood's stories. The story that I was reading in the tub the other night reminded me of a story that I have long wanted to tell.

Some years ago a young man from Maine came to our town to take a job in the university. He was a tall, quiet young man, and we used to see him walking along the walks of the campus or along the corridors of the university buildings carrying great armfuls of books. He did not talk much to the other men who worked in his department in this university and sometimes they would discuss him among themselves, these other men, and make joking remarks about him, or laugh when they saw him go by, his arms laden with books. Then, a few weeks ago, I heard that the young man from Maine had been arrested for stealing books and sent to prison. At the time I thought that he was simply a common book thief and forgot the matter. But since then I have heard more of the story of this man from Maine, and I know how dangerous it is to make judgments about other people and the lives they lead.

There was one man in the department who did not laugh or make joking remarks about Harry—this was the name of the young man from the state of Maine. This other man's name was Wally and he told me Harry's story one day while we were walking after lunch to the bank where Wally kept his money.

Harry, Wally told me, as a boy lived on a farm in the state of Maine. Early in the morning he would get up and milk a hundred cows. When he had finished milking the cows he would clean

17

their stalls, put fresh fodder in their racks, and wash the floor of the barn. In warm weather he would then lead the cows to pasture, and in winter, when it is very cold in Maine, he would leave the cows in the barn and go do various jobs about the barn and the farmhouse. In the evening he would lead the cows back from the pasture and milk them again. Or if it was winter he would stop what he was doing and go to the barn and milk them. Then he would clean their stalls again, put more fodder in their racks, and once more wash the floor of the barn.

When men came in a truck to collect the milk which they planned to sell in the city Harry would help them put the heavy milk cans in the truck. He would listen to their stories of the city. Often, Wally told me, Harry would want to ask the men questions about the city, what it was like there and who the people who lived there were, but he was afraid that they would laugh at his ignorance of city life and so he kept silent.

After he had been a friend of Harry's for a long time and had listened to his accounts of life on the farm in Maine, Wally learned that Harry had for many years loved books. As a boy on the farm he did not have any books and he was always too busy with the cows to go to the district school but one evening when he was leading the cows home from the pasture to the barn he had passed the schoolteacher's house and had looked in her window. The shades were not drawn and Harry could see the schoolteacher sitting in her easy chair, dressed in a pink chemise and reading a book. What book was she reading, this beautiful young schoolteacher from New Hampshire? Harry did not know, and it was not for a long time that he discovered something about the secret tragedy of her life. Every evening she sat at home with the shades on her windows up, reading her books. The young people of her own age in the neighborhood looked knowingly at one another when she passed and made jokes among themselves about her.

Perhaps it was seeing the schoolteacher sitting in her chair reading her book that made Harry fall in love with books. Perhaps he fell in love with the schoolteacher too. Perhaps it was her love for books that made him fall in love with books. Often,

18

after that, when he was leading the cows home to the barn from the pasture he passed by the schoolteacher's house and saw the light in her window. Sometimes he thought that he would let the cows go on to the barn by themselves and that he would stop and ask the schoolteacher to show him her books and tell him something about what was in them, what she found in them, these books of hers. But he was afraid that she would laugh at him or shut the door in his face and so he did not stop, but kept on with the cows.

Once Harry found a book which someone, perhaps a tramp, perhaps a lonely poet wandering over the hills and valleys of this country, America, had left in the pasture where he led the cows. That night when he brought the cows back to the barn he took the book with him, hidden under his rough shirt. After he had milked the cows and washed the barn he went to his attic room and there by the light of his little oil-lamp he looked for a long time at the book, wondering what words were in it, and if there was anything in it about him, Harry. For many nights after that he would look at the book and wonder what the strange black print said, what stories it told.

One day the cows took sick and the next day all of them were dead of a disease which often attacks cows in the state of Maine. That night Harry started walking along the road to the city, carrying his book with him. As he passed the school-teacher's house he saw the light in her window and felt a little sad to know that perhaps he would never see her again. Would she go on like this, reading books for the rest of her life? Harry wondered about this as he walked along the dark road to the city.

After walking for several days he arrived at the city, Port-land, and on the street saw one of the men who had come to the farm to get the milk in their trucks. When Harry told him—this man who brought milk in his truck from the farms to sell in the great dairies and cheese-factories of Portland—about the cows, the man offered him a job. The next day Harry went to work in the dairy, washing milk cans for many hours a day and helping the men who had brought milk from the farms to unload it from their trucks. At night he went to his small room in a boarding house and there he would sit for hours, looking at his book. On his first pay day Harry spent part of the money which he received for unloading and washing milk cans for another book which he had seen in the window of a store where books are sold in the city of Portland, Maine. Harry took it home with him, and that night he looked first at his old book, then at his new one, then at both of them. After that he bought a book on every pay day and spent many hours every night looking at them, wondering about them and what the words in them said.

The other young men who lived in the boarding house in this city of Portland wondered what Harry did all by himself in his room, night after night, and sometimes they made coarse remarks in his hearing, but he did not answer. He wanted to tell them or the landlady about his books, have them come to his room and look at these books of his, but he felt that they would only laugh at him. Many nights he could hear the other young men in their rooms, laughing or joking, and sometimes he could hear the giggles of young women whom the young men had brought into their rooms when they thought the landlady was asleep. They did not know, these young men, that the landlady also heard these sounds as she lay wide awake in her bed at night, and that she wondered what the young men were doing with the young women they had brought into her house. She wanted very much to ask them, and perhaps to be invited to one of the rooms where so much laughter was to be heard, but she was afraid that she would be rebuffed or be turned aside with a cruel joke. And so Harry sat in his room looking at his books and sometimes half-listening to the sounds from the rooms of the other young men, and the landlady lay awake in her bed listening and wondering at the nature of this thing, love.

This young man, Harry, worked for several years in the dairy in Portland. The other men who worked at the dairy, rough men who handled the heavy milk cans as though they were feathers, invited him sometimes to join them after work in trips to saloons or to the brothel which in that city was not far from the dairy. But Harry always refused their invitations, and they would stand in little groups about the dairy talking about him and laughing at his refusal. "He is afraid of drink," they would say, or, "He is afraid of women."

These other men at the dairy did not know about Harry's books and of course he did not tell them. Of all the men at the dairy only the man who had given Harry the job knew about the books. He found out about them one day when Harry was sick and could not go to work at the dairy. That day this man, whose name was Carl, went to see Harry in his room and while he was there he saw the books. He asked Harry about them, and after a while Harry told him, but Carl did not laugh. Often after that when Harry was sitting by himself during lunchtime at the dairy, eating his lunch, perhaps a ham sandwich, perhaps a cheese sandwich, perhaps a slice of apple pie or an apple, with a cup of milk from one of the great tanks in the dairy, this man, Carl, would come and sit down with him for a few moments and ask him about the books. It was during one of these conversations that Harry discovered that Carl had at one time known the schoolteacher from New Hampshire, and had wanted to be her lover, but had not asked her because he had been afraid that she, this schoolteacher, would laugh at him. Thus Harry found out, as he told Wally many years later, something about the tragedy of the schoolteacher's life.

One day Carl sat down by Harry at lunch and told him that he had heard of a great university in the west where there was a need for men who knew something about these things called books, and he urged Harry to send in his name for a job. He offered to write the letter for Harry, who had never learned to write during these years on the farm and in the dairy, and finally Harry agreed. Three weeks later a letter came from the university offering Harry a job and he asked Carl to write a letter for him accepting it. The next day he said goodbye to the other men at the dairy and to the man, Carl, who had helped him get the job, and left Portland for the university town in the west.

Thus it was that Harry had come to our university, Wally

told me. When he had finished telling me this story I could understand many things which I had not understood before. I could understand why Harry always walked about with his arms full of books, and I could sense in a dim way what these books meant to him. And I recalled a scene I had witnessed some weeks before Harry was sent to prison for stealing books from the university library. On a certain day, perhaps Tuesday, perhaps Wednesday or even Thursday, I had been walking in the downtown section of a city, Chicago, which is near the town where our university is. That day I had seen Harry from a distance entering a store. When I came nearer I could see that it was a bookstore and as I walked by the store I looked in. There I saw Harry with a large book in his hand, a book which he had taken from a bookshelf in the store in this city, Chicago. Harry's eyes were shining and he seemed to be trembling. At the time I had thought that perhaps he was ill, perhaps something in the dust on the book had made him sick. But since I have heard Wally's story I am sure that it was not illness or sickness, but some much stronger feeling. Harry did not see me watching him, and at last I walked away. Now that I have heard Wally's account of Harry this scene often comes back to me, and I wonder about Harry in his cell at the state's prison, what he is doing there, and whether they allow him to have books. Do the people who run these prisons of ours understand such things, or do they laugh when Harry says he would like to have a book in his cell? When I find out perhaps I will know more about this life of ours.

1949

22

Short Life of Byron

NORTHWESTERN UNIVERSITY
Department of Sewage Disposal

21 November 49

Dr. W. W. D.,
Department of English,

My dear Dr. D.,

I fear I may have been a little misleading in my note to Dean Shanley. The acoustical oddities of the Northwestern Apartments dining room enable one sitting at the small table in the southeast corner to hear conversations in *all* parts of the room. Thus I was fortunate enough to "take in" the brisk and witty interchange between you and Dean Shanley regarding one or two recent volumes of a biographical or semi-biographical nature. As a result I am very happy to be able once more to supply information which may be of interest and even of use to you and the Dean, for although my own subject is a highly technical one, I am not one of those scientists who go home after a gruelling day amidst the inhuman equipment of the laboratory to waste themselves on such trifling pursuits as bridge, comic books, salad tossing, woodturning, or aluminum spinning.

For me, as for you and Dean Shanley, the Liberal Arts are indivisible, and how is the scientist with his lifeless gadgets to become *a full man* unless he takes the trouble to find out something about those great documents which we call literature? But I am a busy man, frequently exhausted by the day's occupations, and unfortunately less able than I should like to be to settle down for long quiet evenings with some monument of our cultural heritage — possibly *The Mill on the Floss* or *The Seasons* or *Gondibert,* works in comparison with which the tawdry fiction and verse of our own despairing age fades to naught, or worse. So it is that I am always on the lookout for books at once distinguished and brief, in which I may find perfectly distilled the essence of this or that great mind. Such a book is *Twenty-four Lives* by Z. Cedric Yarrow, the British novelist and essayist, and I am delighted to be able to call it to your attention or your attention to it, as the case may be — all the more because it so well fits Dean Shanley's requirements that such a volume be (a) short and (b) full of letters. Mr. Yarrow's book is a scant thirty-seven pages long (including the preface), and is packed with letters to, from, and about such diverse personalities as Byron, Keats, Beddoes, Sir Richard Burton, Jesse James, Keats ("reconsiderations"), Rabelais, Marco Polo, Hazlitt, Robert Falcon Scott, Prester John, Kotzebue, Pope Joan, the False Dmitri, Lamb, and many others, including Keats (in a third and definitive essay).

A striking feature of this work, by the by, is a device which the German critic Luitpold von Esel has called "eingebautesdurchblaettern" or (to rough-cast it in English) "built-in skimming." The author, in short, saves you the trouble of doing your own skimming! The advantages of such a device should be apparent even to Macaulay's schoolboy — who, I am told, has recently become a junior member of the Northwestern English Department. And add to this achievement the author's admirable success in realizing his purpose, as set forth in the preface, of finding a style which is "lucid not to say pellucid, crystalline, transparent, clear, at once chiselled and lapidary, as masculine as Dryden, as feminine as Jane Austen, as neuter as Ruskin, serious rather than flippant, which respects all that is fine in the great tradition of English prose and shuns those perversions of our precious mother tongue to be found in such modern so-called writers as Joyce, Faulkner, Lawrence, and others too numerous to be worth mentioning." To all this I, for one, say "Amen!"

I have copied out for you Mr. Yarrow's essay on Byron, to give you a taste of his style and manner. I would, for various reasons, rather send you the second essay on Keats (in which certain conclusions arrived at in the first essay are revised, in the light of new evidence). This piece runs to hardly three-quarters of a page, heavily leaded and with wide margins; it consists of a single jewel-like sentence by Mr. Yarrow, the utterly right subordinations of which would warm your heart, plus a letter from Keats to Fanny Brawne in which the poet asks rather good-naturedly for the return of a telescope he had lent her, before going on to a few random but imperishable and heartstringtugging reflections on Life and Poetry. But Byron was the author whose name came up in your talk at lunch, and the essay on Byron it will be, despite its (for Mr. Yarrow) rather excessive length. However, misgivings or no, as my old French teacher Professor P. used to say in his impeccable Terre Haute accent, *"vogue la galère!"* — "damn the torpedoes!" (I only hope to God as I ramble on that Dean Shanley — to whom I am taking the liberty of sending a copy of this — is still with me!)

Faithfully,

A. T. S.

Byron (by Z. C. Yarrow, M. A. Cantab., D. Phil. Oxon.)

George Gordon, who was in his eleventh year destined to become Lord Byron, sixth baron of that title, was the son of a debauched father. When nine years old he wrote as follows from Harrow to his mother, the former Catherine Gordon, a native of the oddly-named town of Gight:

Dearest Mumsy,
    Thanks ever so much for the crabapple savories. I have eaten them all and thought them ever so yummy. Tell Cook she must make ever so many more when I come home for the long vac. Hayford Minor has fleas. Condit Major was caned last Friday for playing with himself and sent down last Monday for stealing sixpence ha'penny from the scullery. I have read all of Horace again and Mr. Douglas says my Latin verses show grate [sic] promise but he is not happy about my English verses. Reginald Chadwick Southwick-Northwick, the Captain of the School, mocked my club foot last week and I flang [sic] him in the river.

Yr. loving son,
Gordie

25

Many years later, by one of those curious coincidences of which life offers so many instances, Byron, while traveling in Italy, once more encountered this same Reginald Chadwick Southwick-Northwick, now a captain in His Majesty's Fifth Invincible Fencibles. The results of this encounter are described in a letter which the poet (as he had by this time become) wrote to the Countess Guiccioli, his Italian mistress:

Carita mia,

You will be overjoyed to learn, my darling, that I have found a quack in Ravenna who promises a certain cure for the pox. Only be patient, *bellissima.* While walking in Rome some days past I chanced upon a British officer who was none other than the captain of my old school and my sworn enemy. You may imagine the delight with which I flung him into the Tiber! I must close now for the horses are waiting to carry me to Siena.

Passionately,
B.

When first in Italy Byron was rather contemptuous of the natives, for reasons to be mentioned later, and alluded to them as "the Italians, those soft Latin bastards!" Later this phrase reappeared, strangely transmogrified in the way poets have of strangely transmogrifying, as a line in his poem *Beppo*: "I love the Italian, that soft bastard Latin." Here it would seem that Byron is *praising* the Italian *language,* which — as he goes on to observe in a metaphor richly suggestive of his experiences — "melts like kisses from a female mouth."

Chapters IV-XIX. Skimming.

Hm-hm-hm — Cambridge, unlike Milton not known as Lady of Christ's — hmhm — attacks Scotch reviewers, wit and daring shown here — and so on and so on and so on — travels in the Levant — hmhmhm — takes seat in House of Lords, the irony of this — etcetera etcetera and stuff — marries Miss Milbanke — so forth and thingamajig — separated from wife leaves England — hmhm — Childe Harold — etcetera and so on — in a single night seduces all four daughters of the powerful *antipasto* king — forced to flee Rimini for his life, on this occasion makes remark about Italians mentioned above — hm hm let's see where are we now oh yes — begins Don Juan —

fiddle faddle and so forth — now writing dramas — stuff and stuff and etcetera — aristocratic contempt for Leigh Hunt, amusing anecdotes about this, Hunt really something of a bounder — hm hmhm etcetera — enormous European popularity despite conservative British disapproval, young men wearing hair and collars à la Byron, amusing but significant too — hmhm hm etcetera and so forth and stuff — sympathy for Greeks in their struggle for independence — hm hm hm — arrival at Missolonghi.

On a windy night in April, 1824, Byron wrote the following letter from Missolonghi to his former London landlady, Miss (later Dame) Zelda Fitzleonard:

Madam,

It is with the greatest astonishment that I learn, madam, from an English traveler newly arrived at this place that you have had the monstrous effrontery to sell the three dozen bombazine undershirts which I left in your safekeeping (as I then thought!) on my departure from a country which I have long since learned to scorn for its canting hypocrisy! But most unendurable to me, madam, is the fact that you sold them to Colonel R. N. Southwick-Northwick of his Majesty's Fifth Invincible Fencibles, a person whom I spit upon! Be assured, madam, that upon my return to Italy once I have served the glorious cause of Greek freedom, I shall at once proceed to place this matter in the hands of my solicitors. We shall see then, madam, whether English justice is in fact past all hope!

Yrs., etc.,
Byron

But this struggle, so fraught with symbolic overtones, between the pilgrim of eternity and Miss Fitzleonard, the very paragon of maidenly British respectability, was destined never to take place, for on the day following the writing of this letter Byron was dead from the fever which killed him! His body was returned to England and there buried in the ancient family property of Hucknall Torkard in Nottinghamshire. Whatever gods may be must indeed have chuckled at the irony of it all!

The End

1949

Academic Letter of Recommendation

Dear Professor Mosher:

I am very happy to reply to your letter of January 29th regarding Mr. Desmond Pitcalfe, who has been in correspondence with you about a possible instructorship at Northwestern.

Mr. Pitcalfe has had a distinguished record in English studies both as an undergraduate in Harvard College, where he received his B. A. in 1944, and as a graduate student. As a member of my seminar two years ago he wrote a brilliant paper on the identity of "Stella," arguing most plausibly that "she" was in fact Alexander Pope. I had hopes at the time that he too would go on to further work in the eighteenth century, but he chose the Renaissance. He will complete during the spring term his thesis on "The *Summa Contra Gentiles* and the Minor Poems of Chittiock Tichborne."

I am convinced that Mr. Pitcalfe will be an excellent teacher, and that your department will find him a most congenial person. He possesses, in addition to his impressive command of English literature, an extraordinary range of cultural interests. He speaks perfect Finnish, and during the leave of absence last year of Professor Aalvooaa Haakuninnen taught the Harvard and Radcliffe courses in Finnish. His hammered-brass ashtrays and salad bowls have won high praise from connoisseurs in Boston and New York. He has a sound knowledge of needlepoint, composes songs to which he plays his own accompaniments on the virginals, and owns the second largest collection in Cambridge of records of fourteenth and fifteenth century music. In his senior year he was table-tennis champion of Lowell House, and to his other accomplishments has recently added a mastery of that dangerous and treacherous vehicle, the unicycle.

Two year ago Mr. Pitcalfe was married to Miss Mfwanwy Cabot of Boston, a member of an ancient and distinguished family, and a crack pilot, horsewoman, and racing-car driver, who for the past five years has held the All New England woman's squash-racquets championship. I know that you will find Mrs. Pitcalfe a charming addition to your circle, once you have become adjusted to a certain brusqueness of manner, rather disconcerting on first acquaintance.

Such a letter as this would, of course, fall short of entire candor if it only mentioned virtues and failed to mention possible shortcomings. I am aware of none on the basis of personal encounters, but have heard in a round-about way that Mr. Pitcalfe is a little inclined to epilepsy, occasionally given to taking small girls into empty garages and toolsheds, and a bit of a *voyeur*. Whether such allegations are well-founded or not, I do not know; all I can say is that to err is human, and that if Mr. Pitcalfe does not have these particular weaknesses he no doubt has others.

I hope that this brief note has supplied you with the kind of information which you had in mind. In conclusion I can only repeat that I am delighted to be able to recommend Mr. Pitcalfe without reservation. He will, I am quite sure, be a credit both to Northwestern and to Harvard.

Very sincerely yours,

Albert Trewcott Snard

1949

Gaëtan Fignole: Pages de Journal
Introduction, Notes, and Translation

I. *Introduction*

The dispatch was laconic, the names not unpredictably
askew. A newspaper somewhere—in Pittsburgh, or in Omaha—
ran it under the head, YAWL IN SQUALL—DIES. It read:
"FREJUS, France, July 25—Gaston [*sic*] Fegnoule [*sic*], French
author and writer, drowned early today when his yawl the
Alphonsine II foundered in a sudden squall off this port. The
body was recovered towards evening, somewhat damaged by
sharks."

One doubts whether many readers of the two or three
American papers which bothered to publish the "item" really
stopped to wonder who this "Gaston Fegnoule" might be:
after all, the country was obsessed at the time with, possibly,
Rita Hayworth. It was a hot summer too, and then, the races
were tight in both major leagues. As for Gaëtan Fignole himself,
he would have been less surprised than indulgent at the stu-
pendous indifference which greeted his passing.

For indeed, taking one consideration with another, few
contemporary authors have enjoyed so striking an obscurity
as Gaëtan Fignole, although few have at the same time summed
up more richly the elements of that tradition which has made
France securely French. He was, to be sure, not a prolific writer
as these things go in a country where the artist is still loved and
respected and honored and made much of[1] rather than shunned,
alienated, relegated to signing autographs for clubwomen in
department-store book sections: his pre-posthumous publications
included a scant four novels, none of them conspicuously
cyclical; eight rather casual plays; two small volumes of critical
essays; an inconclusive sheaf of verses; a collection of maxims

---

1. Someone, Professor Peyre or Professor Fowlie, or someone, has pointed out
that "the recent death in Paris of Paul Valéry, in July 1945, became an event of
national significance."

jotted down during a voyage to Marrakesh in 1919; a few dozen almost slapdash *comptes-rendus;* translations of three cantos from a minor Bulgarian epic;[2] and the customary esthetic of the cinema. Of these works only one—the short novel *Rongée (A Woman Gnawed)*—has appeared in translation on this side of the Atlantic, where it attracted restrained enthusiasm in the limited circle of readers who care for that sort of writing.

Fignole lived by choice in a decidedly unfashionable quarter of Paris, not easily accessible to the trifling body of admirers who turned up now and then to pay him homage; on rare occasions he was to be seen at the Café Bled, usually at the cracked table in the murky corner. Of the very few published accounts of his appearance and manner, the most dependable may after all be Edouard Lorenzo's:

> Fignole is rather brown-haired, if anything, with pale blueish eyes which appear to reject the light. Dressed invariably in an ancient mustard-colored tweed jacket and unpressed grey flannel trousers, and never without a pipe which he is forever lighting and letting go out and lighting again and letting go out again, he suggests rather some British younger son who has gone in for breeding pigs, or perhaps an American professor—of English, or philosophy—than the unknown yet all the same illustrious French man of letters that in fact he is. It is in his handling of the pipe especially that he recalls the American professor, as he chews it in grave and silent detachment until "the moment of truth"[3] arrives when, thrusting its stem like a dagger under the noses of the chatterers, he finally cuts the metaphysical knot in which everyone else is all tied up.[4]

Over the years Fignole was at one time or another a symbolist, a fourierist, a dadaist, an existentialist, a neo-existentialist, a jusquauboutist, a royalist, a surrealist, a jemenfoutist, an

---

2. Fignole learned Bulgarian while still a student at the Lycée Landru in Toulouse ("the Harvard of Toulouse"), at a time when the study of that language had not yet become fashionable. In later years he sometimes wryly remarked, "If I had known it would be a bandwagon, I would never have jumped on it."

3 A term derived, one imagines, from the tragic ritual of the bullfight.

4. Edouard Lorenzo, in a paper first read over transatlantic telephone to the Great Lakes local, Modern Language Association of America, at their annual Balzac's Birthday picnic (Petoskey, 1934).

anarchist, and a legumist, and while not notably devout he had for more than thirty years never failed to attend Easter Mass, usually two or three pews behind François Mauriac. He was in his quiet and rather snobbish way the friend and confidant of most of the great names of his time in France, although we may I think take with a grain of salt Professor Ratchet's overbold assertion that he was Proust's model for Zosime de Perpignan.[5]

It was as a *lycéen,* or perhaps earlier, that Fignole began to keep the diary in which for the rest of his life (and in the style to which Edouard Lorenzo has referred as "tellement quotidien!") he was to record his day-by-day activities, his conversations with various personages, and his reflections on the arts and the world. From time to time over a period of forty or fifty years brief excerpts from this diary have appeared in French reviews, but Fignole with firm modesty refused to allow the publication during his lifetime of the entire *journal. "C'est un rien"* ("It is a nothing") or *"Ça sera pour la postérité"* ("That will be for posterity") was his invariable response to publishers who urged him to what they described as a patriotic duty. *"Qu'un français ne veut pas faire publier son journal, voilà une infamie!"* ("That a Frenchman does not wish to have his diary published, that is an infamy!") a certain distinguished *éditeur* once angrily exclaimed. But Fignole was not to be shaken, and beyond an occasional duel from which he invariably emerged the victor, he paid little attention to insults or innuendoes, other than occasionally (in this or that novel or play or *compte-rendu)* to portray his critics in rather grotesque attitudes.

Since his death, however, extensive passages from Fignole's

5. W. W. Ratchet, *A Glance at Wordsworth with Some Divagations on Proust,* 483. The passage in Proust may be worth citing here: "It was in the course of that same night through which I stood silent and shivering, knee-deep in an icy puddle, listening to the voices in the garage—a night from the consequences of which I was to suffer for many years to come—that I became aware, as one becomes aware of these things at such moments and under such circumstances, that the other voice in the garage, the voice which was not Odette's, was not the voice of Swann, but another voice which I would not for several years, and then only by chance and in the course of a masked ball to which I had been reluctantly invited by Madame Verdurin, recognize as the harsh, imperious, yet somewhat fruity voice of Zosime de Perpignan."

32

diary have been appearing in *Les Temps Morveux,* and quite recently has come the announcement that the complete work will soon be issued in sixteen large quarto volumes. One awaits impatiently this intricate record of French literary life, from Zénaïde Fleuriot (who was among other things Fignole's godmother) to the quite youthful Ambroise Tocard, whose poems one critic[6] has called "the warped faces of a clamorous tomorrow."

We are greatly privileged to be able to reproduce here, through the generous permission of M. Claude Fignole, brother and literary executor of the writer, a few *pages de journal* which may be of special interest to American readers. The contribution of French critics over the past century and a quarter or century and a half to a sounder understanding by Americans of their own literature is, of course, at this late date incontestable: we cannot overlook or forget Baudelaire on Poe, Jean Giono on Melville, the elder Marius Broussaille on Fitz-Greene Halleck, the younger Dumas on the Connecticut Wits, Zola on Emily Dickinson, Gide and Sartre on Faulkner, Henri-Marie Frip on Clyde Fitch, Bernard Fay on Franklin, Asmodée Cagoule on the Southern School, and others.[7] Fignole's place in this company is not an entirely spectacular one, nor would he have wished it to be: his knowledge of English was in some respects limited, and his indifference to it considerable. But the observations embedded in the following pages, scattered and casual as they may be, remind us once more and with particular force of the justice of Harrison Fenwick's observation: "A Frenchman is at every moment of his life a critic, in one sense or another, so to speak."[8]

6. Lyndon Dasher, in *Unacceptable Essays.*

7. To this list might be added, for example, André Levinson's description of Thornton Wilder, recently quoted in *The Saturday Review of Literature,* as "that rare avis, someone writing in English and who possesses the Latin sense of form."

8. This remark of Fenwick's was first overheard by the author of these notes in the club car of the Advance Commodore Vanderbilt; again during an intermission of *La Tosca* in Saint Louis; and yet again in the tourist lounge of the S.S. Standish J. O'Grady during a moonlight cruise on the Bay of Fundy. It is here printed for the first time, with the kind permission of Dr. Fenwick.

We regret exceedingly that considerations of space forbid our reproducing all the excerpts in the original, for the benefit of those readers who prefer to get at the language of Bossuet and Céline directly, rather than through the (at best) fogging and distorting medium of a translation. But we are happy to be able to print in French as well as in English at least the first of the entries with which we are here concerned.

II. *Pages de Journal*

21 Mai, Paris. Levé trop tard. Déjeuné à la maison. Décidé que, somme toute, n'aime pas les huîtres frites. Trouvé une molaire qui branle. Sale temps. Alphonsine[9] a téléphoné, son mari a évidemment escamoté la caisse encore une fois. Quel salaud! Mais heureusement il y a toujours l'assurance contre les vols. Relu Polyeucte. *Un pneu[matique] de Gide, qui me demande l'emprunt de mon smoking. Passé l'après-midi tout seul au Jardin des Plantes. Les singes, ressemblent-ils plus aux hommes que les hommes aux singes? Question assez singulière et que l'on ne saurait résoudre comme ça! Trouvé abandonné sur un banc du J. des P. un livre, que j'ai rapporté. Soirée chez Montherlant, qui a raconté quelques histoires sur les taureaux. Avant de me coucher relu* Le Neveu de Rameau. *Observé vers une heure du matin que la molaire branle toujours.*

May 21, Paris. Got up too late, Lunch at home. Decided that, all in all, do not like fried oysters. Found a loose molar. Dirty weather. Alphonsine[9] telephoned, her husband has evidently made off with the cash box again. What a rotter! But fortunately there is always the theft insurance. Re-read *Polyeucte.* A special delivery from Gide, who asks for the loan of my dinner jacket. Spent the afternoon alone at the Jardin des Plantes [a

---

9. Alphonsine Ploc was Fignole's mistress during the final decade and more of his life. The allusion here is to the small poultry business in which she and her husband, Auguste Ploc, had been set up by the writer. The irresponsible conduct of Auguste Ploc, frequently mentioned in the diary, was a constant source of torment and embarrassment and anguish and annoyance to Fignole.

kind of zoo in Paris]. Do monkeys resemble men more than men do monkeys? Quite a singular question and which one could not resolve like *that!* Found abandoned on a bench at the J. des P. a book, which I brought home with me. The evening at Montherlant's, who told various stories about bulls. Before going to bed re-read *Le Neveu de Rameau.* Noticed towards one a.m. that the molar is still loose.

May 29, Paris. Up early. Bored. No word before noon from Alphonsine, who yesterday received an abusive telegram from A[uguste] P[loc] in Marseilles. Rainy all day and my cough is worse. Hasty note from Gide, who has taken the dinner jacket to Avignon. The molar still loose. Looked idly into the book I found on the bench at the Jardin des Plantes. *"Nevada"*[10] by Zane-Grey. In English I would think. Possibly American (noted word "California"). Read one or two passages. Vast and brutal landscapes. Possibly the subject for a *compte-rendu* is to be found here. Alphonsine came to tea, much agitated. Re-read La Fontaine's fables to her, but to no avail.

June 8, Paris. Telegram from Gide in Morocco, where he thoughtlessly took the dinner jacket. Threatening letter from Auguste. Lunch with the Archbishop, who spoke disapprovingly of my ideas for a book on the monkeys at the Jardin des Plantes. Re-read *La Princesse de Clèves.* What perfection! No change in the looseness of the molar. Dinner with Mauriac, who did not quite agree or disagree with the Archbishop. Alphonsine has disappeared [*Alphonsine disparue*] but think she has gone to the

---

10. Zane Grey's "Nevada" was first published in 1929 or sooner. It is the story of Jim Lacy, known to his dearest friends, the brother and sister Ben and Hettie Ide, by the nickname "Nevada," although Lacy is a Texan. Ashamed of his violent past as one of the notorious gunman of the early West, and fearful lest his friends discover it, "Nevada" flees them and becomes a cowboy in Arizona. The Ide family, for reasons of their mother's health, leave California for Arizona, where they buy a ranch and suffer from the depredations of rustlers. Jim Lacy (under that name) cultivates the rustlers and becomes known as one of them, but only in order to destroy them. Near the end of the novel he kills the leading rustler, who has been a sinister threat to the Ides, and only then is it revealed to the Ides that the notorious Jim Lacy and their old friend "Nevada" are the same person. The work ends with "Nevada" gazing at the sunset glow upon the rapt face of Hettie Ide.

country to bargain for guinea hens, for which the market is looking up. This evening glanced again at the *"Nevada"* of Zane-Grey, and found myself inescapably seized by it. Who is this Z-G? A man? A woman? An American, in any event [*en tout cas*], I am sure by now. Telephoned Sartre, perhaps he would know, but he is out of town and his butler refuses to say where. All the same, what vigor! what pervasive brutality! Evidently the new world has some things to say about death! Wonder if *Les Temps Morveux* would take an article? Has Z-G written other works?[11] Haunted by this question and by the molar fell asleep while re-reading *Britannicus*.

June 11, Nice. Arrived Nice this morning with Alphonsine, who insists that I help her arrange the release from jail of A. P. Midi enormously lovely! Auguste surly and insolent on our visit to the jail. Gide answers by wire from Suez that he has never heard of Z-G; fear he suspects my question was simply to cover anxiety about the dinner jacket. Still haunted by the Zane-Grey, which I brought with me on the train. Thoughts of it intruded incessantly upon my re-reading of Pascal. One suspects that in this strange work the American character has found a shatteringly precise statement. Ah, these savage puritans! Fear I shall not sleep well tonight, the molar quiet, but Z-G plagues me and Alphonsine has the sniffles.

June 17, Nice. Still at Nice. Encountered Cocteau on the beach this morning, we discussed Zane-Grey whom he too had not read or heard of. A. P. still in jail, but Alphonsine has not given up hope. Read in *Éclaireur du Soir* that Gide is journeying to the headwaters of the Nile! Obsessed by this strange American work of Zane-Grey, so monstrous in its fashion, so frightening! Have these people souls as we understand souls in our old Europe? Have not been able to complete my re-reading of *Les Lettres Persanes*. In Z-G's fable of cowboys and criminals what horrors are not apparent! One recalls, somehow, Aeschylus, at

---

11. Other works by Zane Grey are *Riders of the Purple Sage, Heritage of the Desert,* and *Ken Ward in the Jungle.*

any rate nothing French [*rien de français*]. Must remember that Cocteau told me "nevada" means in Spanish "snowy." Thus one senses the frigid purity to which the new world pretends! But what splendors of style, though one hardly knows whether to call it prose. Dreamed last night that the monkeys of the J. des Plantes had somehow changed places with the curious figures of Z-G. My nightmare woke Alphonsine, who sobbed until morning. Molar seemed less loose today.

June 27, Paris. Alphonsine and Auguste once more together at the poultry shop and order finally restored! [*tout est rentré enfin dans l'ordre!*] Our good French order [*notre bon ordre français*] of which there is little trace in Zane-Grey. But what a devil of a job getting Auguste out of that jail in Nice; fortunately the police superintendent was, like me, a godson of Zénaïde Fleuriot. The molar turned slightly in its socket about noon. After lunch to the Café Bled for a few hours, where I overheard several young Americans who seemed to be chattering about the problem of evil and the tragic sense of life. Ventured to ask their opinions of Zane-Grey, but perhaps their English was not clear to me, or my French to them. But what a country is theirs, all the same! evidently it is true that there [*là-bas*] one despises and ignores the man of letters!

July 3, Paris. Wakened by telephone call from Alphonsine, who told me joyously that yesterday's receipts had exceeded all previous ones! How happy I was for her and for all of us who have engaged ourselves in this poultry business. While lunching wrote Gide as follows:

> *Cher collègue,*
>   Forgive, I beg of you, dear and much esteemed colleague, my writing to you about matters of the utmost unimportance, when you are at this very moment, perhaps, contemplating in an ecstasy which it would be a sacrilege to venture to imagine, the superb panoramas of the Blue Nile. I hasten to reassure you, admired master, as I am confident that you will hasten to be reassured, that my letter is not on account of the dinner jacket, which is yours to wear as long as you like. I shall not need it in any event before the reception at the Elysée on the 9th of October. It is sufficient honor and reward

for me that you, free to choose any dinner jacket in Paris, have chosen to choose mine!

I regret very much that you do not know the American writer, Zane-Grey, whom I mentioned in my unfortunate telegram of some weeks past. One talks often in Paris of the formidable literature which the America of these days produces and of its effects on the young [*les jeunes*], and I have too long neglected it, I confess. But I am desolated to discover that no one, *no one!* is familiar with the work of this extraordinary genius who, masking his deepest thoughts with crude images of the "Far-West," exposes a surpassing awareness of the hopeless and despairing violence of the new world, its feverish concern with sexual purity and its almost sexual concern with sudden death! The hero "Nevada" (of whom the true name is Jimm Lacy) I see as someone much resembling an American Orestes, haunted by an anglo-saxon sense of guilt which drives him at once away from and ineluctably towards the young lady, so ominously chaste, his ideal beauty, and who is named Hettie Ide.

And imagine [*figure-toi*] a work in which the hero and his friend refer to each other with casual callousness as "old panther!"[12]

I had hoped, my old one, that you might lead me to other works of this writer of whom, apparently, no one has heard. But I am happy to be able to introduce you to this volume, so sinister, even menacing [*menaçant*], and which suggests in its own fashion the gulf between this Europe and that America.

Again, I beg of you, give yourself no concern about the dinner jacket; if I should like to have it back, it is rather for reasons of tradition (my father wore it as assistant mayor of Toulouse!) than on account of the cost. I would write at greater length but am bothered by a loose molar which makes composition difficult. Alphonsine is of the happiest, and would, I know, insist on being remembered to you. The poultry business is flourishing, there are regular orders now from three embassies! and the profits exceed all expectations. Our old France will find a way out, eh? [*Notre vieille France se débrouillera, hein?*]

Ever thine, Ga-Ga [*Toujours à toi, Ga-Ga*][13]

---

12. Fignole's occasional uncertainty with English betrays him here: evidently he is referring to the frequent use in "*Nevada*" of "pard" or "old pard" (in the sense of "pal" or "chum"). The older sense of "pard" ("leopard," "panther") was almost certainly not intended by Zane Grey, but Fignole may not have had access to Harrap's large English-French dictionary, in which both senses are given.

13. "Ga-Ga" (from "Gaëtan," presumably) was Fignole's nickname among his friends.

July 19, Paris. At last have finished the *"Nevada"* of Zane-Grey! What an experience, almost an ordeal! One recalls Dante! But this happy ending, so profoundly cynical, so striking a comment on the gelid ideal of the puritan! What influence it will have on my own future work I cannot say now. Perhaps I shall ask Camus to predict this influence in an article, perhaps I shall predict it myself in the interview which I have promised M. Edouard Lorenzo. Attempted at lunch to re-read *Bérénice*, but Racine savorless [*sans saveur*] and very 17th-century after Z-G. Auguste has once more made off with the cash! A violent scene with the theft insurance people; I was shaken for hours afterwards! It is their sort of scepticism and lack of faith which may wreck us all! Alphonsine crushed again. Sartre still out of town. Mauriac abruptly changed the subject when I mentioned Z-G at lunch yesterday. How melancholy I feel! The molar has flared up again. Have decided to escape it all for a few days' sailing. *July 22, Toulouse.* Once more in my own country! [*dans mon pays à moi!*] But in Paris a heartrending departure from Alphonsine, who wished me to go with her to Antwerp where Auguste is now in jail. Told her of my arrangements to visit Toulouse, to go sailing, but she accused me of denying the fact that I exist, of fearing to engage myself, to involve my destiny with the destiny of all men. Haunted on the train by these words of hers! Can I be yielding thus to the influence of "Nevada," who also attempted to run away from his existence? What fate awaits me as I sail from Toulouse to Fréjus? Took water and seabiscuit aboard Alphonsine II this afternoon. Weigh anchor tomorrow dawn. Brought with me two books: the *"Nevada"* of Zane-Grey and the *Oresteia* of Aeschylus, works so remote from each other in time and place, one Greek, one American (of which the Greeks would have had no idea!), one ancient, one modern. Yet who is to say that they are entirely different? Deposited my will with a notary of Toulouse. Have left dinner jacket to Gide, a quarter-share of the poultry profits to Athalie.[14]

---

14. Fignole's wife.

July 24, on board Alphonsine II. Weather clear, with slight quartering wind. How peaceful is the immensity of sea and sky, how immense their peace! Tied the tiller down all morning to busy myself with the diary and with thoughts of this dear Zane-Grey [*ce cher Zane-Grey*]. That dratted molar [*cette foutue molaire*] lost overboard during the night: must one see this as an omen? Thought of Alphonsine alone in Antwerp. Mild sunstroke about noon. Towards dusk found a lamprey in the scuppers, and with the addition of candle-drippings and barnacles achieved a magnificent *bouillabaisse* over the spirit lamp. One is not French for nothing! [*On n'est pas français pour des prunes!*][15] Superb sunset! Reading Aeschylus and Zane-Grey alternately as the light failed. Curious dream last night: a new arrangement of counters in the poultry shop. Must write Alphonsine.

July 25, on board Alphonsine II. Landfall shortly past sunrise. Will there be word at Fréjus from Alphonsine? from Sartre? from Gide? from Mauriac? from Montherlant? from Camus? from Cocteau? One cannot say. During the night a book took shape in my mind, Zane-Greyish, perhaps, but, of course, French to the bottom [*Zane-Greyesque, peut-être, mais, bien entendu, français au fond.*] Wonder whether it would be quite wise, after all, to tell Sartre about Z-G before I have finished my own novel? Possibly not. A slight rash from the lamprey, but this was to be expected. Wind freshening. Could "Nevada" have found in his Arizona views of sea and sky so magnificent as these? One is led to reflect on the nature of space. Must tell Picasso. Dull throbbing in the empty molar socket. Fréjus now off the port bow. My article (to be published before the novel) will begin somewhat as follows: (title) *Ce qu'on trouve chez Zane-Grey: réflexions sur l'Amérique de nos jours, ou le roman "convulsif."* [*What is found in Zane Grey: reflections on the America of our time, or the "convulsive" novel.*] (first paragraph) In reading Zane-Grey, an American author less well known among

15. According to widespread Toulouse legend, Fignole's grandfather was the inventor of *sauce fignolade*.

us [*chez nous*] than he deserves to be, one is to begin with forced to consider. . .

[This is the final entry in Fignole's diary. Following the last words printed here, the handwriting becomes indistinguishable, degenerates into meaningless squiggles. One can only assume that Fignole "went down writing," as it were, stubbornly intent, in the very teeth of the squall which destroyed him, on completing the sentence in which at this, the ultimate moment of his life, he had become involved. The inexpensive notebook in which he kept his *journal* was still grasped tightly in one hand when his shark-mauled body was retrieved, a pencil stamped "A. Ploc & Cie., Volailles de Marque" in the other.[16] His interlinear edition of the *Oresteia* turned up, badly waterlogged, in the foundered hulk of the yawl. But there was no trace of "*Nevada.*" One supposes that it sank slowly to the bottom of the sea, or that it was washed ashore, perhaps, in some deserted cove or sparsely-settled inlet of that ancient rocky coast, there to be found by a simple sailor or peasant or fisherman to whom its underlinings, its marginal comments, its very language would be quite meaningless!]

1950

---

16. These facts were mentioned with great tact and eloquence by Asmodée Cagoule in the funeral oration which he pronounced before the relatively tiny crowd which followed Fignole's coffin to its last resting-place in the old cemetery of the family parish of Sainte Agrippine at Toulouse. Fignole's death occurred soon enough for this oration to find a place in Cagoule's recently-published *Oraisons Funèbres Diverses (Sundry Funeral Orations),* under the title "À la revoyure, brave Fignole" ("Farewell, worthy Fignole").

Canto 101

That year the beached ships sank deeper in the sand,
Timbers warping, paint peeling, the cordage rotting,
Everywhere the dull stains of Fe_2O_3, when the sun was bright.

V tot god osennaya pogoda. And with the autumn weather
compelled. Gentlemen, said El Presidente,
What is your pleasure. All this dead wood now. I want a faculty
Now I want a faculty that will put this university
ON THE MAP. bolitos. As much as we can get.

I will now entertain a motion to adjourn, said El Presidente.
In April the cruelest month, wie gesagt, came the announcement
of a new heaven and a new earth,
these things being proclaimed by Ser Ernesto, con gli occhi onesti e
tardi:

    first quarter: essays instead of novels
    second quarter: novels instead of essays
    third quarter: asses instead of navels
To your posts, men! cried Ser Ernesto. Fiat lux, ruat coelum!

Everyone turned out for the department meeting that year:
gente attufata in uno sterco,
Longinus Minor in the chair. Un col capo si di merda lordo.
In the meanwhile Douglas had published fifteen articles six notes
twelve rejoinders and a review of Fungus's new book.
Professor Fungus has done us all a service
supplied a long-felt need. His discovery
that Wordsworth was circumcised sub rosa
in a night ceremony at Saint Botolph's
By the Archbishop in person, with a pair of garden shears,
the prepuce snatched to heaven by flights of angels
compels the revision of all our prevous etceteras.
Haw, said Longinus Minor. HAW.
I thought some of these articles quite good. Haw.
But a few of them I think lack bolitos, Douglas.
Say whatever you will about Fungus
he's got bolitos.

In the senescence of the year, buried in books, Hayford sought the
truth
quaecumque sunt vera. Huddled in his carrel, recalling
the Cave of the Winds at Niagara, cursing inventive Vespasian,
aware of the ewig weibliche. Dans mon pays il fait temps pluvieux.
Crouching suffering reading. Regretting:
Thus Hemingway's prose replaces
Melville's bolitos.

That month a rune stick cast upon the shore
polubolitines thalasses
was brought to Professor Sparsus for deciphering. The angular scratches
on what seemed to be a well-polished hambone
defied for several weeks the ingenuity
of that best of scholars, Messire Giovanni.

I think, he opined, it may be the description
of a journey made to Lapland in the spring of the year 908
by two Danish scholars, to collect Laplandish bolitos
in the form of coprolites.
But I cannot be sure of course without further study.
On the other hand it may (as I strongly suspect)
be an order for lutfisk sent by a housewife of these parts
to Johnson's Fish Shop, and somehow gone astray.
I don't doubt that I shall be able to get a small book out of it.

Longinus Minor noticed the buds on the trees.
Spring comes slowly up this way. But in any case
employing all the devices for efficient and rapid communication
of a mechanical civilisation, his voice reaching everywhere
eni Troiee eureie, as well as points east and south,
hired himself a handful of new instructors, well versed in to kalon:
Launcelot Gobbo, George Tesman, and Lord Osric their names.
Osric preferred the ballet but was fond of opera too.
Tesman, said Fungus, is a man of considerable culture,
speaks a few words of Arabic, owns ten thousand classical records,
Weaves his own undershirts according to an antique pattern,
And in his spare time practises the toreutic art.
His wife I believe is Aristotle's niece.

43

Gobbo's dissertation on Pope's debt to Lady Winchilsea
or Lady Winchilsea's debt to Pope or whatever it may be—
well, anyhow, Gobbo's dissertation has won him much esteem
among the big men in the profession. Sherburn thinks
it has plenty of bolitos.

On a table in the Grill someone had incised with the tine of a dime-
                                                                store fork
"Elsie loves Bergen Evans." And below it in a different hand
"dia phobou kai bolitou ten ton toieuton mathematon katharsin."

Just string along with western culture, son,
and you can't go wrong,
said Fungus the Phoenician, fifty years dead more or less.
In this life, my boy, you'll never get enough bolitos
live as long as you will. *But get all you can!*

Oed'und leer der Herr.

                                                    1950

44

$_7N^{15} + {}_1H^1 + {}_6C^{12} + {}_2He^4$

"James could not, of course, have foreseen the hydrogen bomb."

Oswald Alving stopped typing and for three minutes studied the sentence. Then he x-ed it out, and typed:

"James could not have, of course, foreseen the hydrogen bomb."

Again Oswald stopped typing, and, contemplating the new version, absentmindedly re-lit his pipe. Only the muted snarl of a neighbor's vacuum cleaner made the summer air angry (this a line from his novel; how he had worked to get it right!). All well up to now. The first eleven pages of this draft lay in a rough parabola beside his chair. Glancing down at page one, he read contentedly the opening sentence of his essay:

"We have, perhaps, yet to meet Henry James on his own terms."

This was fine: "perhaps" had given little trouble, barely enough to remind Oswald of his responsibility as critic. But *placing* "of course" might easily take what was left of the afternoon. Somewhere he had read, "for clarity's sake, not peace but the sword is necessary in the kingdom of literature." How well said! If only *he* could have said it as well!

No one to turn to for help, either: his wife simply didn't give a damn about either Henry James or matters of style, and Clifford Pyncheon was out of town, lecturing at Yale and Syracuse on "God and Poetry"—or was it "Poetry and God"? How easily things came to Clifford Pyncheon, how adroitly he had moved over the years from Plato to Marx to Freud to Myth and God! But Myth was already going somewhat out of fashion: Clifford had begun to smile a little when the younger instructors mentioned It. How about God? What would Clifford's next move be? No need for bitterness, though: leave that sort of thing to Bob Cratchit. One learned a lot from Clifford Pyncheon, however meanly one might envy his ease in conversing with Jesuits at lunch. As for Bob Cratchit—no hope there! He would simply suggest, sneering, that "of course" be omitted altogether:

"James could not have foreseen the hydrogen bomb."

Oswald winced to think of the bald phrasing. What had led Bob Cratchit to the kingdom of literature anyhow?

Oswald's pipe gurgled slightly. The summer air was washed with sudden stillness, as the vacuum cleaner stopped. How would the sentence sound if quoted by another critic?

"...but if Mr. Alving is wrong about James, he is wrong so much more boldly and rewardingly than anyone else has known how to be that it would be a shame to hold it against him. No serious student of James (and any other kind of student may safely be ignored) can afford to overlook the implications of 'Henry James and the Carbon Cycle,' in the Fall number of Fungus, *and particularly of Mr. Alving's comment, 'James could not have foreseen, of course, the hydrogen bomb'."*

Oswald typed out all three versions of the sentence:

"James could not, of course, have foreseen the hydrogen bomb."

"James could not have, of course, foreseen the hydrogen bomb."

"James could not have foreseen, of course, the hydrogen bomb."

The pipe went out, and Oswald tapped the ashes into the large flower pot which Maud Osric had given him for an ashtray. Maud? Possibly. She would certainly be more sympathetic than Bob Cratchit, though less wise than Clifford Pyncheon. How smoothly Clifford alluded to Aquinas! Maud could not do *that*, though she had tried. Yet she would at least *understand* Oswald's problem. But would she be willing to *leave* it at that? She was quite capable of arguing that James *had* foreseen the hydrogen bomb, or if not the hydrogen bomb at any rate the atom bomb. Oswald could see her now, tossing her mop of red hair in that quick vivacious way and challenging him pointblank to deny that this or that sentence in *The Princess Casamassima* was anything but a veiled prophetic allusion to atomic fission or fusion.

Too bad that Alex Osric insisted on discussing Maud, in her presence, as though she were his favorite novel. It was Alex, as a matter of fact who had first described Maud as "tossing her mop of red hair in that quick vivacious way," and since then Maud had tossed and tossed her increasingly moplike hair in a way that new members of the faculty (at least those from Arkansas and Nebraska) found more disconcerting than vivacious. And *could* Maud, if she wanted to, *really* write better than Elizabeth Bowen? Much the same, no doubt, but *better?* Yet these were disloyal thoughts: it was to Maud that Oswald had turned almost instinctively on discovering that another critic had used the sentence he had been saving to open his Melville essay:

"America must come to terms with Herman Melville."

Only Maud's faith during the long months that followed had prevented Oswald's destroying his notes for the essay and cynically presenting his first edition of *Billy Budd* to Bob Cratchit. And it had only been with her encouragement that (after rejecting "America must come to grips with Herman Melville") he had finally achieved his new opening sentence:

"Our world continues, at its peril, to evade what is most his own in Herman Melville."

If only he taught at Columbia and felt free to drop around and put the problem to Jacques Barzun! But he did not teach at Columbia, and he could not be sure that he had even seen Jacques Barzun. He could not be sure, because the person who had pointed out Jacques Barzun to him was Bob Cratchit, and the pointing-out had taken place in Chicago, where Oswald and Cratchit were strolling between trains while on their way to a Modern Language Association convention.

"How do you know it's Jacques Barzun?" he had asked Bob Cratchit.

"Because it looks like Jacques Barzun."

"How do you know what Jacques Barzun *looks* like?"

"Why, nobody could look as much like my idea of what Jacques Barzun looks like and not *be* Jacques Barzun."

The conversation had gone on like that for a few minutes

more, very unsatisfactorily. Just another example probably of Bob Cratchit's silliness. Would he ever learn the difference between being witty and being merely silly? Clifford Pyncheon, for example, was *witty*. But all this aside, Oswald had for a long time been thinking how satisfying it would be if he could only work into the foreword to *Hawthorne's Urgencies* a thank-you to Jacques Barzun, a kind of *ex voto* offering one might almost say:

"...and such merit as the book may possess is owing in very large part to them. I am particularly indebted to so-and-so, so-and-so, Maud Osric, so-and-so, Robert Emmett Cratchit [a lie, but it might shame Bob a little], *Clifford Pyncheon, so-and-so, and most of all, perhaps, to Jacques Barzun, who from the beginning has given generously of his patience and his wisdom."* Possibly a little commonplace, but the details could be straightened out once the book was written.

Oswald looked again at the three sentences. Odd how this sort of thing always gave the most trouble: what was really *central* came into focus almost of itself; it was invariably "of course" and "perhaps" and "possibly" and "however" and "after all" and the parenthetical "I think" that hung one up. Yet small as they were, they were indispensable, like the pituitary gland or a sanctuary lamp. Did everyone engaged in the act of criticism have the same trouble with them? Oswald glanced at his bookshelves, with their files of *Fungus* and *Peristalsis* and *The Dakota Quarterly* and *Oestrus* and *The Panther's Nostril* and *Jackpot* and *Umlaut*. Were the critics who filled these files bothered by such problems—critics like William Crimsworth, Harold Skimpole, Amelia Sedley, Jack Horner, Paul Dombey, to name a few? Again Oswald set to typing:

"James could, of course, not have foreseen the hydrogen bomb."

This might do; there was something about it that hauled you up short. What was it Jack Horner had written about the tactic of shock? Studying his own sentence, Oswald recalled faintly a sentence from Paul Dombey's note on Faulkner in last quarter's *Oestrus:*

"One can, of course, not overlook the fact that Faulkner's world is, after all, not Dante's."

But no one could possibly accuse him of stealing from Dombey! One might as well accuse Dombey of stealing from Skimpole— although, come to think of it, Stanley Edgar Hyman *had* accused Dombey of stealing from Skimpole. Or had Hyman simply accused Dombey of idiotically misconstruing Skimpole's notion of drama as symbiosis? Or was it *Skimpole* who was Hyman's idiot in this instance? Oswald could not remember, and there was no time now to make sure: through the closed study-door he heard his wife whistling. Dinner about ready apparently. Why must she always whistle just at dinnertime? And tonight that party at the Cratchits'. He thought of the note about himself which he had imagined for the "Contributors" page of *Fungus:*

"Oswald Alving has abandoned teaching for writing, and is now living in a cabin in the Grand Tetons, where he is at work upon a critical study of Hawthorne. His novel, The Occluded Front, *is scheduled for Fall publication."* The note was just about as he wanted it, though the cabin would be out of the question for a long time. He began typing again, and had typed *"James, of course..."* when his wife rapped on the door.

"Dinner!"

"All right. Be there in a minute."

"Well, don't *wait!* It's waffles."

"Oh, all *right!*"

Waffles for dinner again! The third time in two weeks! What had come over the woman? One could just imagine Clifford Pyncheon feeding waffles to a Jesuit! Hastily Oswald finished typing the interrupted sentence:

"...could not have foreseen the hydrogen bomb."

More hastily he typed:

"Of course, James could not have foreseen the hydrogen bomb."

And still more hastily:

"James could not have foreseen the hydrogen bomb, of

49

course."

Seven versions in all. These last three not too good: no tension. Get all possibilities down though. This the moment of decision. Yet with the smell of waffles seeping into the room the final choice would have to wait. The plight of the critic. Or was it true that *plight* was going out of fashion too? Had Clifford Pyncheon had to endure this sort of thing while he was writing *Into One Ball?* How comfortably Clifford could refer to himself as "a sort of lay Trappist." He might have been a real one too, if that attack of shingles had not laid him low just long enough to give Thomas Merton a head start. So Clifford had remained in the world, with his jolly Jesuits and an occasional grave Dominican.

And the Cratchits' party! Bob Cratchit being silly not witty. Or sneering at Kierkegaard. Whom he had not read, of course. Whom he had, of course, not read. Agnes Cratchit making unpleasant jokes about Clifford Pyncheon. The Osrics engaged in mutual admiration. Once again the muted snarl of the neighbor's vacuum cleaner made the summer air angry. *Would* "made angry the summer air" have been better? Who in God's name could be cleaning at this hour?

Absurd under the circumstances even to dream that anyone might ever have occasion to publish the dust-jacket biography which was to begin:

"One of the most distinguished of the younger critics, Oswald Alving, who was born in 1911, spent the first ten years of his life within the walls of the Rhode Island State Penitentiary, where his father was, in prison parlance, a 'screw' or guard. 'It was those years,' Alving has remarked, 'which gave me my first real sense of the human situation...' "
Or that any critic would ever write:

"But these are minor objections; the important thing is that Mr. Alving has finally consented to make all his essays available in a single volume. And it should be evident by now to everyone but the drabbest positivist that Mr. Alving is, after all, the best of our younger critics. Indeed, one notes the publication of Deserts

50

of Vast Eternity *with something approaching that humility which Mr. Alving himself so eloquently urges upon us all. Is our centerless culture really so deserving?"*

* * *

"One hesitates, as it were, to label with such a confining word as 'system' Mr. Alving's extraordinary fusion of Longinus, Plotinus, Aquinas, Jung, and certain notions derived, one supposes, from Harold Skimpole . . . the most satisfying definitions, by far, of 'tradition' and 'poetry' (in the larger sense) that any critic has yet given us."

* * *

"It is in his study of James in particular that Mr. Alving goes as far beyond, say, Clifford Pyncheon, as Pyncheon himself (the Pyncheon, that is, of Into One Ball) *went beyond the Paul Dombey of* Rear-Guard Action *or the William Crimsworth of* A Cracker Manifesto. *'James,' writes Mr. Alving (in the well-known essay which has already become a sort of modern classic, 'Henry James and the Carbon Cycle'). . ."*

Again the fateful knock on the door. Like the horn in *Hernani*. Would that allusion be too sticky to use somewhere...?

"Your waffle is getting *cold!*"

"All right, all right! I'm coming!"

1950

Furioso's Nosegay of Critics

"What is it like to be a critic?" "If you had it all to do over again would you do it all over again?" For a long time *Furioso* has had it in mind to put these and similar questions to two or three dozen of our leading critics, but what with even graver issues always turning up, it was not until fairly recently that the decision was made to "fire away." *Furioso* thereupon requested its good friend, Jack Churchmouse, to draw up a list of critics and to shoot letters at them, and he was happy to oblige.

Mr. Churchmouse is strikingly well qualified for such an undertaking. Not that he is a professional man of letters—far from it. Indeed, for several years following his graduation with distinction from Williams College, he devoted himself exclusively to working his way up in the family business—for three generations Milwaukee's largest missal-bindery. But the time came when his youngest brother, Wendell, Princeton '47, could take over the ever-expanding enterprise, and Jack was able to give up the daily grind for more congenial pursuits. Since then he has "made something of a hobby," as he shyly phrases it, of cultivating the acquaintance of critics, in much the same way that other people in his set cultivate ball-players, traffic cops, bartenders, and jockeys. Thus when *Furioso's* call came, he was ready for it, and sitting down to his desk he immediately dispatched letters to Kenneth Burke, Allen Tate, Lester J. Fiddler, Buddy Empson,[1] R. P. Blackmur, T. S. Eliot, John Crowe Brooks, and various others. Several months having passed without replies from Blackmur, Burke, Tate, Empson, Fiddler, Eliot, Brooks, and some of the rest, and a deadline ineluctably approaching, *Furioso* decided to go ahead and publish the answers that *had* come in, hoping that the delinquents might thus be shamed into writing.

---

[1] Possibly a confusion with Buddy Ebsen, the dancer. Churchmouse is occasionally more impetuous than accurate. [Ed.]

Given Mr. Churchmouse's personal friendship with each of the critics, several of whom had spent many long, talk-crowded nights or weeks in the private bar of his Lake Shore Drive *garçonnière* or his Bucks Country *pied à terre*, a mere form letter was, of course, not to be thought of. But to each warm chatty personal note were appended the following questions, in addition to those cited above:

1. Roughly speaking, how did you happen to "go in" for criticism?
2. Are you inclined to feel (a) hurt, (b) angry, (c,d) scornfully or indulgently amused when someone appears to be insufficiently *serious* about the things that you are *sufficiently* serious about? For instance, Original Sin. Hot Jazz. The Devil. Criticism *itself.*
3. Do you make any special preparations for engaging in the act of criticism: i.e., lying down for a few minutes beforehand, beef tea, prayer, mental fantasies, raw eggs, whiskey?
4. Are you at present or have you ever at any time been a member of the Boy Scouts of America?
5. List, if you will, a few of your hobbies.

The replies to Mr. Churchmouse's letters are printed below. While it has been necessary, for reasons of space, to dock some of them a little, *Furioso* is persuaded that, by and large, nothing of crucial import has been omitted. Take it away, Jack Churchmouse and critics!

Letter No. 1. Moody P. Greensleeves.

Dear Jack,

Your letter arrived just as I was putting together a few ideas for a rather similar "round up" that *Peristalsis* is planning, and I fear it would not be quite fair if I let *Furioso* get in ahead of them with a statement of how I function as critic. So, reluctantly, I must turn you down. On the other hand, you know pretty much where I stand on all the central questions, and I'd have no objection if you wanted to do a little piece about me on your own. Perhaps something in dialogue form might catch many of the people who read *Furioso*.

53

I'd be happy to look it over and suggest revisions.

I am sending you under separate cover a complete list of my articles to date; you may have missed two or three of the European publications. It was good to hear from you. Elsie and I will be delighted to give you a drink whenever you are in this part of Delaware. We are living on twenty-nine acres down here which Elsie's father left her. She is still passionately absorbed in breeding beagles, and after 13 years is finally beginning to sell a few of them. I have no "hobbies" in the strict sense of the term, although I do help to water the beagles occasionally on weekends.

P.S. Did you happen to see Hyman's reference to me in the *Tallahassee* as "less ignorant than most critics of Boker"? His article in general is not bad, although I'm not convinced that Stanley is more than half right in calling Ned Branny's style "glutinous." I wish I could get Ned and Stan together for a talk some time.

* * *

Letter No. 2. Mungo Fick.

Dear Jack,

. . . and I'm exceedingly grateful that you saw fit to include me in your list of "some of the better critics of our time writing in English," though I think you may be a little rash in placing me with Mr. Burke, Mr. Blackmur, Mr. Tate, and a few others, but I shall quarrel with you about that when I see you; is there any chance of your being in Camden in the near future? I'm sure that some of the people at Princeton would be glad to come down and give you a few of their ideas. . . What you are aiming at, I take it, is something on the order of a group of statements that *Peristalsis* is getting together, to be, I think, called "The Critic in the Mirror"—in fact, I know that is the title, because as it happens I've just sent a piece off to them and frankly I'd hate to do the same kind of job all over again, although it isn't that I have anything against *Furioso*. . . . In general, as you, I take it, may be aware, my method of getting *at* a novel, in the more usual sense of "novel," is primarily through. . . [Here Fick's letter is interrupted, *Furioso's* loyal but literarily incompetent old cleaning woman, Maxine, having used the backs of the second and third pages for an unusually heavy laundry list.]

* * *

Letter No. 3. H. Vincent Bulkington.

[*no salutation*]

Evidently my remarks to you in San Diego last September 9th failed to make fully clear to you my opinion of you and your crowd!

54

Do not for a moment imagine that I am alluding to the *Furioso* review of my book on Joaquin Miller! You already know my contempt for that performance, which was, if possible, an even more rotten display of malice than the review in *Peristalsis*. It is increasingly apparent to me that both *Furioso* and *Peristalsis* are "fronts" for certain cynical forces bent on destroying all that is great in our western tradition in general and our native tradition in particular. . . Thus, if I seem angry now, it is not for personal reasons, but for infinitely wider and deeper reasons. Did you think to flatter and wheedle me by placing me on the same list, though well *below!* Burke, Blackmur, Eliot, and the rest of that sinister crew? Point out *one* name on your list, besides my own, of a *native* west-coast critic! The party line is only too obvious to me!

The answer which I gave *Peristalsis* I give you now, with as much disgust for your insolence as I can muster: *"No!"* I might add that I am sending copies of this letter, together with a full account of the whole conspiracy, to *The Saturday Review of Literature*, J. Donald Adams, and Senator Kefauver.

P.S. Please cease sending me sample copies of *Furioso!* I will *not* subscribe!

P.P.S. My wife has read this letter and fully concurs in these sentiments, in the event that you are flattering yourself that your fulsome remarks about her[2] have succeeded in turning *her* against me too!

*   *   *

Letter No. 4. Marshall Creap.

Dear Jack,

For Christ's sake! What kind of [*deleted*] is *this*? "Some of the better critics of our time writing in English"! Granted, Jack, that Eliot and Tate might rate such billing, or possibly Fiddler, or Heilman, say, at least for his six or eight best explanations of Warren's novels, all the same how can you justify including guys like Fick, Abner Vest, and Ringbolt? Sorry, old man, no can do. The truth is, I just bit on the same kind of bait and damn near killed myself. So if you want the dope on how *I* see *me* you'll have to dredge it out of *Peristalsis;* they bulldozed me into some god damned symposium or round-up or other they're running. In fact, Tony Footless got downright petulant about it, and since he may take my piece on Auden, the Last

---

[2]The sole allusion to Mrs. Bulkington in Churchmouse's letter was as follows: "Please, by the by, give my best to the incomparable Gladys. If I thought that all Welshwomen were as beautiful and that they were half as well able to preserve their beauty as she, I might take a jaunt to Wales myself one of these days. But the years have been more than kind to both of you, as far as that goes."

Western Man, I figured I might as well play ball... If you have nothing better to do than read my contrib. to this *Peristalsis* deal you'll probably recognize one or two phrases which I've been meaning to thank you for Jesus knows how long.

That "hobbies" question of yours is a killer! I stick to bourbon myself, but I hear that Abner Vest has been hitting the needle lately. . . Did you know that Ned Branny's second boy flunked out of Dartmouth?. . .

* * *

Letter No. 5. Daniel W. Ringbolt.

Dear Jack Churchmouse,

It was good to hear from you after this long silence. Someone was asking me only the other day whether I had encountered you in recent years, and appeared rather disappointed when all I could tell him was that I had heard rumors of your being seen with some of the *Furioso* people.

As for your request, I cannot, of course, to begin with, accept your flattering implication that I am one of the better critics of our time writing in English, if I recall your phrase correctly. I do appreciate your good intentions. But even if I felt up to answering your questions, I fear I could not undertake to do so. The fact is, I am engaged on a quite similar statement which I have promised to *Peristalsis,* and you know how sensitive Tony Footless is about duplication of articles. I am, as I have intimated, not persuaded that anything of this sort which I might have to say is deserving of publication, at least for the moment, although I do think such a harvesting of ideas is in general an excellent thing. . . .

I have been wondering—this is, of course, between us—about some of the names on your list. Why Creap, for example? I am by no means the first person to ask, "Where would Marshall Creap be today if Mungo Fick had not been so inexcusably negligent in letting his notes on Bramwell Bronte lie around the beach .that summer at Far Rockaway?"[3]

_____

[3]It may be worth noting here that Creap and Ringbolt have been at odds ever since they appeared together on the famous tape-recorded round table, "The Critic's Navel," in the winter of 1949. On that occasion Ringbolt accused Creap of having munched a crisp lettuce and bacon sandwich on toast right through his (Ringbolt's) best "lines," with the result that the stenographer who transcribed the recording for publication *thought* she heard Ringbolt say, "Erie's total park system is a blot on a fine nation," instead of what he actually *had* said—"Aristotle's remarks, I insist, do not *define* imitation." The proofreader who allowed this slip to pass into print fell back on the feeble defense that in the context of the entire round table it made as much sense as any other statement. He was, of course, sacked. [Churchmouse's note.]

Letter No. 6. Abner Vest.

My dear Churchmouse,

Six months ago I might have found your request almost flattering. Today I am only aware of its profound unimportance, and if I have, for reasons of my own, acceded to a similar request from *Peristalsis,* it is not that I regard it as less unimportant. At twenty I became a Communist, at thirty a Catholic, and at forty a New Liberal. I know now how empty all these gestures of mine were. Tonight I leave for a month's rest and meditation at the Buddhist monastery in Scranton; I shall, perhaps, simply stay on there indefinitely, if I receive some aid from the Ford Foundation. Please do not write me again.

P.S. I do not believe that I am acquainted with *Furioso.*

* * *

Telegram No. 1. Samuel W. Albacore.

SORRY PRESSURE OTHER BUSINESS PREVENTED ANSWERING YOUR LETTER SOONER VERY GRATEFUL YOU THOUGHT OF ME ABSURD OF COURSE LISTING ME WITH BURKE MR. ELIOT FIDDLER ETCETERA REGRET ALREADY COMMITTED PERISTALSIS SIMILAR ARTICLE ARE YOU ON FURIOSO STAFF NOW ONLY HOBBIES NEEDLEPOINT AMATEUR HORSE RACE HANDICAPPING SAD NEWS ABOUT BRANNY'S BOY REGARDS.

* * *

Letter No. 7. Timothy Ferret.

Dear Mr. Churchmouse:

Am very sorry to inform you that Tim was killed three weeks ago while fishing off the Florida Keys, he went there to study up on Hemingway, in his dear thoughtless way he tied the fishing line around his waste [*sic*] while eating lunch & a giant baracudda [*sic*] "struck" dragging Timmy overboard. Am sure Timmy would have been happy to answer your questions especially [*sic*] the one about Original sin he certainly was in favor of it and got just furious at those that were not and would not let them in the house, & certainly did hate Positivits [*sic*] tho you know how modest he was and just before leaving for the Florida keys had to force himself to write the same kind of an article for Peristalis [*sic*] which they begged him to write it and did it only because he was so kind & could not bear to refuse to do a favor for somebody that asked him to do one for them. Like Mr. Footless the editor of Peritalsis [*sic*] that wrote and wrote until Timmy finally said O I will do it if he wants it that *much* tho a nuisance. Timmy joked about it but I typed it also all his stories & poems & plays these last few years and think people will think it is

57

wonderful, it is all about Timmy. We were engaged for eight years and were going to be married this coming Thanksgiving if Timmy had not gotten his "Fullbright" thus forceing [*sic*] us to postpone it again, he was my first teacher in freshman English and can still hear him the first day in class explaining the "ironys" [*sic*] in Barbara Fritchy [*sic*], it is dreadful to think I will never hear him talking about Tradegy [*sic*] again & sincerely hope I can meet you some day and we can have a talk about Timmy, he did not have any hobbys [*sic*].

Yours sincerely,
Mary Ann Grosbeak

* * *

Letter No. 8. C. Wilbur Condit-Taylor.

Dear Jack,

My answer must be "No"—for two reasons: (1) I have already promised a rather similar statement to Tony Footless, and (2) as you may, perhaps, not have heard, Lucy has left me, and I have my hands full trying to take care of the children while maintaining at least a minimum schedule of work, including the *Peristalsis* article. I didn't much want to do it; it is a silly and presumptuous sort of undertaking. But I *am* grateful for the opportunity to answer Hyman's charge that I derive my notion of epigones from Burke, although as you may, perhaps, imagine, Hyman did not bother to use a decent word like "derive."

As for Lucy, she walked out one night about a month ago—in fact during the most crucial stage of the second draft of the *Peristalsis* essay, leaving a quite unpleasant short note for me. Since then I have had an equally unpleasant postcard from Albuquerque, nothing more. I had for some time been urging her to see a psychiatrist, as she seemed obsessed with the notion that I had done her some injury— possibly by using money which she appeared to think we had been saving towards a new Bendix to buy those galley proofs of "The Fiddler of Dooney," with corrections in Yeats's own hand. My Yeats book has, of course, been sadly delayed by all this, but you may, perhaps, be happy to learn that I now hope to finish it in August. I have not yet decided on a title; what would you think of *Violence of Horses?* You will, of course, catch the allusion.

As I see it, the primary value to me of the *Peristalsis* article is that writing it has compelled me to scrutinize everything I have done up to now, and I am convinced that my notion of my own work is clearer now than ever before: I *see* it all, that is—by which I mean that it has all come more precisely into *focus*. What has, in the past,

58

been available to my readers has at last become available to myself.

I am glad to hear that *Furioso* is contemplating this sort of undertaking. You may, perhaps, be interested to know that it is one of poor Lucy's favorite magazines.

*   *   *

Letter No. 9. Deming Blue.

Dear Jack,

I wonder if you realize that the people you mention are almost to a man the same people that *Peristalsis* has announced as contributing to its series on "The Critic in the Mirror"? Of course, it probably doesn't matter too much; I suppose any such list is bound to contain many of the same names, though your asking Daniel W. Ringbolt puzzled me, and I was surprised that you had apparently not heard of Tim Ferret's death. I'm not sure yet of all the details, but Marshall Creap has most of them, and from what he says, Ferret was in Key West following up some Hemingway clues, got into a fight in a dive down there with a drunken playwright, and was clubbed to death by the bouncer, an admirer of Hemingway who resented Ferret's bad imitation of Hemingway's manner (I don't know if this means his *literary* manner or just his manner in general). On the other hand, Sam Albacore insists that there was a more sordid aspect to the relations of Ferret, the bouncer, and the playwright, but Creap feels that Albacore may simply be trying to give the affair a fashionable literary turn. I know I never heard *that* about Ferret, though I can't imagine that many people are going to miss him except, possibly, that poor girl he's been stringing along all these years, and I wouldn't be surprised if it turned out that there's something going on between her and Albacore.

I'd like to help you out on this request of yours, though I think you may really be overdoing it by including me on your list. But I'm also on the *Peristalsis* list, and while I suppose I could stall them, it might look funny if I suddenly threw them over and them turned up with the same sort of thing in *Furioso*. Don't misunderstand me, Jack. You know how I mean that.

My God, how long *has* it been since you were last in Yonkers? And a hell of a lot longer since we first met at that freshman smoker at Williamstown—you quoting Housman and me hating Matthew Arnold. What twirps we must have been in those days! I've managed to keep in pretty good shape, though I haven't any real hobbies. You may recall that Dorothy used to coach basketball at Radcliffe, and she still sees to it that I don't spend all my time in my study. Our oldest girl is about ready for Smith. I expect that you in your ivory tower (I deduce the ivory tower from your seeming not to have known about Ferret) hadn't heard that Ned Branny's son was expelled from Dartmouth—running some sort of policy game in the dormitories, I believe. Speaking of Ned, I've just this week looked through an advance copy of *The Whale and the Mule,* that Melville-Faulkner study he's been working on so long. It's a wonderful idea, but Ned is not the man to do it, at least not on the level he's attempted.

Looking over your questions again, I think I'd better tell you before someone else gives you a twisted version of the facts, that I was a member of the Boy Scouts for a short while in the early 1920's, when almost every boy in America over the age of 12 belonged. I expect I was involved in the usual wienie roasts, overnight hikes, knot-tying, and so on, though all that is pretty vague now. But I never took my first-class test, and I could almost swear that I never even became a second-class scout. It's easy to forget how many of us were in the same boat in those days, as I was explaining to young Art Schlesinger at lunch quite recently...

It was good to hear from you, Jack. Again, I'm sorry not to be able to oblige, but I know you'll understand. I wish you were around to advise me if I *do* decide to review Branny's book; I'm afraid it's going to be extremely embarrassing.

P.S. I suppose you wouldn't know any details of the Condit-Taylor mess? Lucy always impressed me as a rather sullen sort of woman, though I doubt Mungo Fick's story that she pulled a knife on C. W. Abner Vest has also disappeared, by the way.

* * *

Postcard No. 1. Anthony Footless, Jr.

Dear Churchmouse,

I've just heard from Deming Blue that you people are planning something very similar to our "Critic in the Mirror" series. I hope the rumor is false, for reasons which I need not, I trust, spell out for you. Forgive my using a postcard for so crucial a message, but the new *Peristalsis* letterheads have been held up; we think sabotage not unlikely. I thought some things in your last issue quite amusing. Who writes the bulletins? Hastily.

* * *

Letter No. 10. Postmark blurred, signature indecipherable.

Dear Jack,

Please do not regard this as a sour complaint because you did not see fit to include me as a contributor to the "Nosegay"; no doubt you had your reasons for omitting me, and no doubt they seemed sufficient to you. Or it may be that the decision was not in your hands. But I could not, out of self respect (if that term is any longer valid in our world), let your failure to include me pass without comment.

I shall spare you my speculations about why you chose to invite certain persons to contribute; I am, as you know, not given to envy, and if I express some surprise at your choices, I do so in the interest of criticism and of poetry, not in my own interest. A man in *your* privileged position would not, I suppose, be likely to feel flattered by, say, the prospects of an invitation to Menhaden Hall,[4] although there are those who might well be beguiled by the twenty-nine acres (or is it thirty-nine?), and the beagles, not to mention Elsie's charitable disposition. I do not, for example, even care to imagine what she may have said about me to Tony Footless; I have no wish to seem a Joseph.

You know my work and, knowing it, have made your choice. Such facts I am prepared to accept, as I am prepared to accept Clara's ankylosis, my uncle Carl's addiction to pinball machines, or the existence of the Devil. I am too keenly aware of my own shortcomings to have time for pointing out those of others, and if it is my lot to be an exile, so to speak, I hope I can face that fact with fortitude, and even, it may be, with some measure of wisdom. I have read my Sophocles.

I bear you no resentment, then, and wish you well in this venture; I only hope that you will not be forced to take the scrapings from *Peristalsis'* table.

1951

---

[4]The name of the Moody P. Greensleeves place in Delaware. See above, Letter No. 1. Formerly the property of Greensleeves' late father-in-law, Talbot K. Menhaden, the well-known manufacturer ("Relentless" trusses, "Dribble" spot remover), art-collector, and bibliophile, Menhaden Hall has enjoyed a long and glorious history. Mortimer Menhaden of Menhaden, the first Menhaden of Menhaden, arrived ten minutes too late to sign the Declaration of Independence, and it is thought that the curse on the house dates from that moment. Oddly enough, the Hall was, during much of the nineteenth century, a frequent refuge for critics: Cornelius Matthews "hid out" there from the Molly Maguires, and it is believed by some Poe scholars (H. Hayrick, E. Shambles, etc.) that Poe wrote "The Fall of the House of Usher" in revenge for the failure of his attempt upon the virtue of the noted beauty, Betsy Furlong, mistress of Menhaden. [Churchmouse's note.]

Mosher, Prince of Swabia

A Tragedy

Characters:

Mosher, Prince of Swabia
Carlo, a gentleman in the service of the Prince
Wallace, a Clown

Act IV, scene iii

(Enter from opposite directions Prince Mosher and Carlo before the castle of Count Roderigo, Lord of the Isles.)

MOSHER: Greetings, brave friend and sharer of my purpose.

CARLO: Greetings, most noble master and my liege.

MOSHER: Methinks this castle that appears in view,
Wall heap'd on wall and lofty tow'r on tow'r,
So that the wren himself climbs not so high,
Nor yet the sable martlet in his pride,
Nor heaven's winged king, the tawny ousel,
Should be, unless sad Fortune plays me false,
The citadel and very seat of him,
Mine enemy and thrice-accursed foe,
One whom I hate as I do hate black hell,
Death and its minions, the Count Roderigo,
Lord of the Isles and master of this realm.

CARLO: I prithee, gentle sire, be not so wroth,
So rash and froward in thy bitter curses,
For I do fear this place conceals no friends
To thee or to thy father, Swabia's king,
And I have heard it said this very day

62

From one that had it from a captain here,
That instant death awaits thee in this place
Should inauspicious stars disclose thy name
To this same lord, the fierce Count Roderigo;
And I agree and heartily concur
That this grave pile and monstrous-seeming heap
May be the count's, and most like doth contain him.
But soft, hark you, my lord, conceal thy visage,
For one approaches, if I do not err.

(Enter Wallace, a Clown, carrying sundry faggots.)

CARLO: How now, sirrah fellow, what house is this? *(points to castle)*

CLOWN: Eh? Beest thou strange folk? Never have I seen beards cut thus. To be bearded by thee bodes no good I fear to me. He-he-he.

CARLO: What house is this? I say.

CLOWN: What *louse,* sir? Nay, if thou playest fast and louse with me, I will not tell thee.

(Carlo, laughing, strikes him, and the Clown groans loudly.)

MOSHER *(aside, to Carlo):*
                Ha! this bumpkin hugely pleases me,
                And willingly would I lend him more ear!
          (to Clown)
                Good fellow, come, give me an answer straight!
                Is this the seat of great Count Roderigo?

CLOWN: My master's seat? Fie, sir, for very shame. Yet come to think on't, how should I not know my master's seat, being as 'twere, sat upon?

MOSHER *(aside, to Carlo)*:
                'Fore God, a pretty witty knave forsooth,
                Albeit he smells so foul of goats and dung,

And wears a beard so like a pigeon's nest.
Most monstrously I dote upon his chat!
But have at him, friend Carlo, I beseech thee!

CARLO   "Sat upon"? Nay, friend, I do not follow thee.
(to Clown): Construe me this same "sat" as thou dost use it.
What manner word is this?

CLOWN: What word, sir? Nay, sir, no word but a turd. For
hark'ee, sir, thus do I construe it, being, saving your
worship, but a construmacious man: your seat, sir,
is but, as 'twere, your bottom, sir, or fundament.
Now this same "sat" is the past of "sit," sir, and
your "sit" is your seat's motion or manner of being.
Thus the past of "sit," sir, is what passeth your seat,
and what is this thing which passeth your seat, sir,
but a turd?

*(Prince Mosher and Carlo laugh heartily, and the Prince claps
Carlo on the shoulder.)*

CARLO: God's bitter wounds, meseems I could endure
To spend a fortnight heark'ning to this clod,
Whose words though rank are shrewd and passing
              wise;
But yet, sire, we must not forget thy purpose,
Which was to seek out vill'nous Roderigo,
For that he hath thine eldest sister ravish'd,
Thy brother slain, thine aged mother spay'd,
Thy youngest sister sham'd, thine aunt dishonour'd,
Thy noble uncle strung up by the balls
To rot unheeded i' th'unfriendly air,
And thy most royal father, Swabia's lord,
Insulted, scorn'd with terms of vile contempt,
And on his white hairs base contumely heap'd.
Oh, sir, the timid dogfish which doth hide
His coward heart from ev'ry passing trout

64

Would, did he but suffer these outrages,
In anger and in furious wrath pursue,
Discover and annul the cruel offender!

MOSHER: Ay, Carlo, there thou touch'st the very quick
And tender marrow of mine inmost grief.
(to Clown, giving him a purse)
Go, friend, and many thanks for this rare sport
Which thy brave wit hath given me this day.

(Exit Clown)

And now, dear friend and cousin, let us seek
Some means to enter and to penetrate
Within the mass and substance of these stones,
Wherein I do suspect my foe doth lurk.
Do thou go that way and I will go this;
Within the hour seek me here again,
And if by chance thou shouldst not reappear,
I then will know it if thou art not here.

CARLO: It breaks my heart, dear lord, to see thee thus,
Whom I have known when youth sat on thy brow
Like to a jocund fly upon a cake;
But banish memory! Work's to be done!!!
Alas, I fear me dreadful deeds in store,
For last night as I toss'd in sleepless dreams,
Methought the hoot-owl buggeréd the bat,
Dank corpses rose from graves and danced a round,
And in the streets grave citizens went mad
And bark'd like foxes at the gauzy moon;
A bleeding maidenhead hung in the air,
Whilst lions litter'd in unbroken streams,
And on the Capitol a tiger farted.
These things are omens, I have been informed
By one that hath entire command of ancient lore.

MOSHER: Farewell, most noble and most loyal Carlo!

CARLO: Farewell, my liege, dearer to me than life!

(Exit Carlo in one direction)

MOSHER *(solus)*:
> And now, God willing, once behind that wall,
> I shall or die or be not dead at all!
>> *(Exit in the opposite direction)*

1951

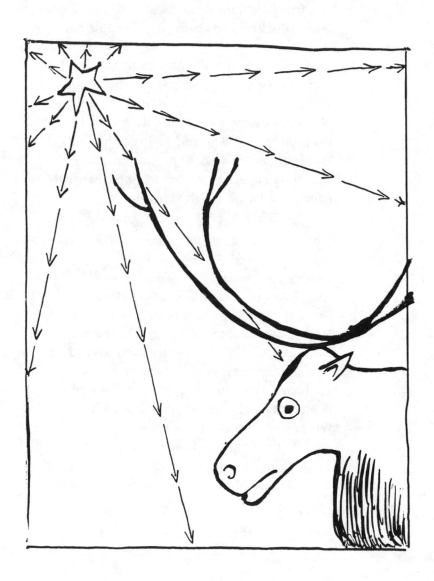

Clutter Counters Everywhere

Many months ago the writer of this Bulletin received a circular letter from the New York *Herald Tribune*. The letter struck him with such force that he immediately ceased the academic routine he had been engaged in when it arrived—tearing student papers into strips, doodling, staring pensively through the window, going for a drink of water, winding his watch, jotting down reminders to himself about the nature of tragedy, poking at a cavity, consulting the dictionary for the meaning of a word he had pretended to understand when a colleague used it at lunch, thumbing through *Time,* briskly bringing his desk calendar up to date—and settled down to think about it (the letter) and what it might portend. He is tired of thinking about it now, and hopes to purge himself of it by getting it into print, together with a few of the questions it has raised.

> Dear Sir: [the *Herald Tribune* begins]
> In these crowded days . . .
>> . . . when 69,392,699 magazines are published each week
>> . . . when busty pocket-books (the latter-day dime novel) clutter counters everywhere
>> . . . when TV is revolutionizing the pattern of American entertainment
>> . . . and when Western culture is facing its greatest threat since Charles V threw back the Turks
>
> are you finding it hard to keep your students abreast of the really GOOD—the really IMPORTANT—books being published in the U.S.? Would you welcome—at no expense to you or YOUR COLLEGE— the weekly assistance of the foremost critics and authors writing today?

(There's more to the letter, but let's stop here.)

Now it's clear, in the first place, that to such questions only a chump or a traitor could unequivocally answer, "No!," so packed are these questions with all that an American holds dear

—overwhelming statistics, the bust on the pocket book (or was this a misprint for *dusty?*[1]), the historic parallel with its flattering implications that the reader knows all about Charles V and the Turks, *plus* a chance to get something for nothing. And when the letter goes on to assert (as it does) that the *Herald Tribune* BOOK REVIEW *Magazine Section* is "generally accepted from coast to coast as THE authoritative publication in the field of literary criticism," the impulsive recipient of the letter is likely to hustle his note of acceptance off to the post office without even bothering to turn out the office lights or straighten his tie.

But the writer of this Bulletin is not an impulsive recipient, or at any rate an impulsive letter-answerer, partly owing to a firmly-rooted habit of not answering letters until months or years have passed, and partly because an early training in scientific method taught him to jump at conclusions *only when he feels like it.* He did not feel like it in this case, preferring (the scientific method churning up in his memory) simply to ask a few questions. There's nothing very systematic to them—you can get just so much mileage out of the scientific method.

(1) Is it really *true* that 69,392,699 magazines are published each week, or did the promotion people at the *Herald Tribune,* working under a terrific pressure to *get the letter in the mail,* simply grab that number out of the air? It is the sort of number that sounds right, as plain round numbers would not, and the writer of this Bulletin is perfectly happy to accept it. But he would like to know for sure before he risks tossing it out at a cocktail party (after painfully memorizing it), only to have the campus precisionist snort, "Nonsense!" or "Rubbish!" in the decisive way the campus precisionist has of snorting these words. Moreover, the campus precisionist is sure to go on and ask something shattering like, "How about certain magazines—*The Hud-*

---

[1]Not likely, given the *Herald Tribune's* reputation for accuracy, and the fact that pocket books are usually placed, *not* on counters, but in racks with plenty of circulation, and are thus less likely to get dusty than to get tattered or dog-eared from being brushed up against people rushing for trains or hurrying to have prescriptions filled.

son Review, for example—which are *not* published each week?" (He *might* ask, "How about *Furioso?*," but being a campus precisionist is not likely to.) Well, how about it? Or doesn't the *Herald Tribune* count non-weekly publications *as* magazines? If not, why not? What sort of big-city journalistic arrogance is involved here?

(2) Is "clutter counters everywhere" a deliberate echo of Joyce on the part of some suppressed genius in the *Herald Tribune's* circular-letter plant, or is it one of those fragments of accidental poetry which the world could ill do without? If it *is* a muted scrap of song by a hidden genius, is this genius also responsible for the rather snide distinction implied in "foremost critics and authors"? Can it be that this genius, heavy with unborn novels and plays, an "author" in his own mind, is getting a bit of his own back (in advance) by this devious belittlement of critics? Would this genius do better to become an English instructor, given his tendency to phrases like "the latter-day dime novel"? At all events, what personal tragedies lie hidden behind the façades of great metropolitan newspapers anyhow?

(3) If the recipient of the letter has a sense of fair play (as every defender of Western culture has, including nowadays the Turks), he's sure to raise some questions about the New York *Times Book Review* and *The Saturday Review of Literature* before he decides to throw in with the *Herald Tribune* crowd. And surely those publications themselves are not going to take lying down the assertion that the *Herald Tribune* BOOK REVIEW *Magazine Section* is generally accepted from coast to coast as THE authoritative publication in the field of literary criticism. (No doubt they have long since let fly with their counter punches, but the writer of this Bulletin is apparently not on their mailing lists.)

All the same, what is a conscientious teacher, the dark splintery corridor outside his office jammed with restless, chattering students demanding to be kept abreast of the really GOOD—the really IMPORTANT—books being published in the U.S.—what is such a teacher to do? Read all three? God forbid!

Read none of them? That way, in our culture, lies loss of face at the very least. One thing he might do, before he goes over to the *Herald Tribune,* is to demand that its critics and authors be able to match or top certain touchstone passages from the publication he is already committed to. For instance, if he is a *Saturday Review* boy, he might ask the *Herald Tribune* if it can come up with anything to equal this from the *SRL:* "In this novel Edward Lyons exhibits certain qualities that may produce a writer who will have enough to say, and who will say it dramatically enough to assure himself a certain future."

Or, he might ask, "How are the *Herald Tribune's* triple-adjectives compared with the following sampling from the *Saturday Review?"*—"revealing, competent, and important," "beguiling, intelligent, and well done," "colorful, provocative, completely absorbing," "absorbing, fast-moving, and plausible," "simple, moving, horrifying," "smooth, unpretentious, dove-colored writing," "dim, well-intentioned, squirming" (this last triplet from a review in which a character is compared to a sea-anemone—what do the *Herald Tribune* people know about sea-anemones?).

If the *Herald Tribune* can tie or surpass these, well and good. If not, let it wheedle and flatter as it will; the canny recipient of its propaganda will stick to his *SRL* (or his *Times Book Review),* Charles V and the Turks or no Charles V and the Turks.

(4) Finally, what about the statement, "at no expense to you or YOUR COLLEGE"? Why "YOUR COLLEGE" in caps and "you" in lower case? Do we have here an instance of the tendency in our society to put institutions ahead of *people?* How about human dignity? Or is the *Herald Tribune* cynically suggesting that the recipient of its letter is the kind of person who will immediately hoof it around to the Chairman or the Dean to present this little scheme for saving money for the college, while incidentally calling favorable attention to himself? *Are* there such persons in American higher education? Or is this an appeal—even more cynical in effect—to some sort of school spirit on the part of the faculty? The answer is not clear, but behind the words we

sense the New York promoter, sleekly and expensively tailored as befits the *Herald Tribune*—yet with all his glossy exterior, his *savoir faire*, his memories of *South Pacific*, a blood brother to the duke in *Huckleberry Finn*, with *his* cynical, "There, if that line don't fetch them I don't know Arkansaw!"

* * *

Better tell those students in the corridor to come back after lunch.

1951

The Human Condition

The drawing room of the Merkles' home in East Burlap, Bucks County, Pa. Late afternoon. REGINALD MERKLE, ELSIE DIEFENDERFER, GREGORY FLACK, and an UNIDENTIFIED CORPSE.

REGINALD

I was down in the cellar patching some screens
When the doorbell rang. It was lucky I heard it.
But let's have a drink. How about you, Elsie?

ELSIE

Of course. Two olives, Reginald,
And no vermouth.

GREGORY

          No olives for me.
As a child I nearly choked on an olive,
And I have hated olives ever since.
That is the reason, in case you have wondered,
Why I shun parties, and prefer the solitude
Of modest bars. I have a horror of olives.

REGINALD

I never knew you disliked parties, Gregory.

ELSIE

Thank you, Reginald. Speaking of parties
I suppose you have read *The Cocktail Party?*
I am hoping to see it next month in New York.

GREGORY

I wish I could remember a few of the things
The critics have written about it. But you know
My memory has always been abominable.

REGINALD

The Cocktail Party? What is it? A movie?
Or a novel? Or a movie made from a novel?
I don't have very much time for reading,
Not as much as I'd like. And I rarely go
To the movies except when a western is on.
You seem empty, Elsie. Another drink?

ELSIE

Of course. Two olives, Reginald,
And no vermouth. How like you, Reginald,
Not to have heard of *The Cocktail Party*.
Although it is really less of a shock
To learn there is something else you have not heard of
Than it would be to learn there was something you had.
Another olive.

REGINALD

      I'm sorry, Elsie,
But I didn't quite catch what you said. I was trying
To fish this olive out of the jar.
All I meant to say was...

GREGORY

      What you meant to say
Is not clear, Reginald. But clarity
Was never one of your virtues—to the extent
That your small merits may be described as virtues.
I am not sure that it would have made much difference
If you *had* read *The Cocktail Party*.

You must excuse my being frank, Reginald,
But you must not think of me as the same person
Who went out of that door at Easter.

REGINALD

Went out? Was carried out, you mean.
Anyhow, all I was trying to say was...

ELSIE

You should know, Reginald, that repartee has never
Been one of your strong points, if I may describe
As "strong points" qualities which in other people
Would be merely defects. *The Cocktail Party*
Is a play in verse by T. S. Eliot.

REGINALD

T. S. Eliot? A T. S. Eliot used to fell steers
Down at the slaughterhouse when I was a boy.
At least I think his initials were T. S.
And I think his name was Eliot, or maybe
It was a name that sounded like Eliot.

ELSIE

I am sure it was not the same T. S. Eliot.

GREGORY

Reginald is incredible! I wish Cynthia were here
To take all of this in. Where *is* Cynthia?

REGINALD

I don't know. Was she supposed to be here?
Did everyone plan to drop in today?
Not that I mind, of course. Thank God
There's plenty of stuff to drink in the house

And I think I can dig up some cheese and crackers.
Has Cynthia read *The Cocktail Party?*

ELSIE

Of course. Cynthia reads everything.

GREGORY

She was a charter member of The Book of the Month
   Club.

ELSIE

She was a charter subscriber to *Time.*

GREGORY

She read *Worlds in Collision* the day it was published
And has had a great time baiting astronomers.
But then Cynthia has always thought
That scientists need to be put in their places...

Enter CYNTHIA TROUT

REGINALD

Hello there, Cynthia, we were wondering if you...

CYNTHIA

Maxwell had an *attack,* and blamed it on some gin
That he'd bought at a bargain, so I decided
To have a little talk with the liquor-store man.
I expect he won't sell *that* brand again!
But where are my teeth? Has anyone seen my teeth?

ELSIE

Oh dear, Cynthia! You're always mislaying them.

75

GREGORY

I will never forget the night of the blizzard
In '39, when you left them in the taxi,
And Ogden sat on them. Where *is* Ogden?

CYNTHIA

In California. Maxwell chose to stay at home
And take his chances with cut-rate gin,
But Ogden is in California. Or at least
Where Ogden is is as much California
As it is anywhere.

To REGINALD

Have *you* seen my teeth?

REGINALD

No, Cynthia. Have you looked in your mouth?

CYNTHIA

Why there they are! How obvious of you, Reginald!
Say what you will, Reginald *is* obvious.
And now, what have you all been talking about?
I am sure you have been talking about *something*.
Something is what people sometimes talk about
Though not always. I have known occasions
When it was nothing rather than something.
I know you may call me a foolish old woman
But I have learned at least *that* much from life.
May I have a drink, Reginald? Brandy.

REGINALD

Sure thing, Cynthia.

CYNTHIA

And some gin for a chaser.

ELSIE

We were talking about *The Cocktail Party*
And Reginald naturally has not read it:
He did not even know what it was, Cynthia.

CYNTHIA

Oh, my dear, you are not as young as you were,
If you will pardon an old woman's frankness,
And it *is* a little strange to find you surprised
At Reginald's ignorance of anything.

ELSIE

I do not mind your frankness, Cynthia:
It has simply strengthened my own convictions.
I have learned a great deal quite recently
That I had never suspected previously
About myself, and about other persons too.
Although Reginald, of course, is hardly a person
In the sense in which "person" can be said to have a
        meaning.
The only T. S. Eliot Reginald knew about
Was a man who once stuck pigs down at the slaughter-
        house.

REGINALD

"Felled steers" is what I said, *not* "stuck pigs"!

ELSIE

What does it matter? The important thing is not
The kind of work he did at the slaughterhouse
But the fact that it was at the slaughterhouse he worked.

CYNTHIA

That is what comes of trusting Reginald
To remember anything correctly! The man
Who worked at the slaughterhouse was T. J. Ellis.
He died in '27 of the mumps.
I am an old woman and sometimes confuse dates
But I am sure it was the mumps. He was past seventy.
The aged do not often survive the mumps:
It is a burden which they must learn to bear.

REGINALD

I was reading an article about that, Cynthia,
I think it was in...

CYNTHIA

Do you imagine
That we are really concerned, Reginald,
With the kind of articles *you* have been reading
Or with the places you have read them in?
Or with what you think? Have you hidden the gin?

REGINALD

It's right there, Cynthia, by your elbow.

CYNTHIA

Please pour me some. *The Cocktail Party?*
Of course I have read it. For a second, though,
Lost between present and past, between memories
Of childhood days spent peering through the chinks
Of the pens at the slaughterhouse, and this moment
My thoughts wandered a little, I am afraid.
Of course I have read *The Cocktail Party*.
What did you want me to tell you about it?
That is, if what you wanted me to do
Was to tell you about it. But where are my teeth?

GREGORY

I believe they are still in your mouth, Cynthia.

CYNTHIA

Of course. How clever of you, Gregory.
But then you always were the clever one.
Reginald was slow, good only at marbles,
And at arithmetic and things like that.
While Gregory was always the clever one.
But someone is missing. Where is Mildred?

REGINALD

Still at her grandmother's in Cedar Rapids.

ELSIE

I never knew Mildred had a grandmother.
She has never spoken of a grandmother.
Least of all a grandmother in Cedar Rapids.

REGINALD

Good Lord, Elsie! You mean you've forgotten...

GREGORY

I thought it strange that Mildred was not here.
I spoke to her only last month on the phone.
She must have left quite suddenly, Reginald.

REGINALD

I guess so. The message came after dinner,
Just as Mildred and I were finishing our coffee.
The doorbell rang, and I went to answer it.
It was a young man with a wire for Mildred
From her grandmother's brother in Cedar Rapids.
That was two weeks ago. I had a postcard,
But you know how Mildred is about letters.

79

ELSIE

You say a young man with a wire for Mildred?
Do you suppose it really *was* a young man
And that what you call a wire was really a wire?

REGINALD

Well, what else...

CYNTHIA

"What else?" Of course
You *would* say "What else?" Reginald. How like you!
But who can tell what forms *they* will put on?

REGINALD

"They"? Who do you mean by "they," Cynthia?

CYNTHIA

Those who bring the messages, of course.
One might I suppose call them the messengers.
And now where are my teeth? I know:
They are in my mouth. What were we discussing
When someone mentioned Mildred? The book of the
          month?
Worlds in Collision? Something new in canasta?

ELSIE

No, Cynthia, it was not the book of the month.
Why should we discuss the book of the month
With Reginald? We were talking about Mr. Eliot
And of course about *The Cocktail Party*.

CYNTHIA

Yes, I remember. I have read the play.
You wish I suppose to know what I think of it.

80

To REGINALD

But do you really wish to know, or is your wishing
Simply one of the lies into which you retreat
To dodge yourself coming around the corner?

GREGORY

That was very well said, I think, Cynthia,
And I am glad *I* did not ask the question
Now that I see what a fool Reginald
Made of himself. But look who's here!

Enter MAXWELL TROUT

REGINALD

Hello, Maxwell.

MAXWELL

Hello, Reginald.

ELSIE

Hello, Maxwell.

MAXWELL

Hello, Elsie.

GREGORY

Hello, Maxwell.

MAXWELL

Hello, Gregory.

CYNTHIA

Maxwell! Oh my dear, I am happy to see you!
Is something the matter? Is it that gin again?

Have you heard from Ogden? Have you seen my teeth?
I am sure I left them somewhere. But *where?*

MAXWELL

They are in your mouth, Cynthia. I see them quite
   plainly.

CYNTHIA

Of course! How observant of you, Maxwell!
But I have always regarded you as observant.

MAXWELL

Where is Mildred? I had thought she would be here.

CYNTHIA

She has gone to her grandmother in Cedar Rapids.
Or so Reginald says. We all know what to make
Of the kind of things that Reginald says.

MAXWELL

Her grandmother? I did not know that Mildred
Had a grandmother in Cedar Rapids. Are you sure
It *was* Cedar Rapids, and not Sioux Falls?
These small Iowa towns are all much alike.
Waking on trains early in the morning
I have often noticed how much alike they are.
Are you quite sure that it was Cedar Rapids?

REGINALD

Of course I am sure that it was Cedar Rapids!
Why shouldn't I be sure?

CYNTHIA

That is a question

82

Which only you can answer, Reginald.
I do not envy you your way of being sure,
But you must find what comfort in it you can.

ELSIE

Only think, Maxwell, Reginald has confessed
That he has not read *The Cocktail Party!*

GREGORY

He thought it was a movie. That is to say
He thought it was what he calls a "movie"—
By which I take it that he means a *film.*

MAXWELL

I am not surprised. That is how Reginald is.
Or how the person Reginald *thinks* he is, is.
I have read the play already several times
And have ordered tickets for the New York production.
It has taught me much about the human condition
That before reading it I had never suspected.
I wish Ogden would read it, but I am afraid
It would only confirm Ogden in his feeling
That he might as well put up with his various vices.
Ogden is one of those who like to be reassured
That they cannot help being whatever it is
They are. Fortunately he is able to afford it.

REGINALD

That's a funny way to talk about Ogden:
Considering, I mean, that he's your oldest friend.

MAXWELL

Your notions of what is "funny," Reginald,
Mean as little as for you to say, "I mean."
Ogden is my oldest friend only in the sense

That I have known him longer than the others.
At Princeton he was my idol, and he supplied
The capital with which I started business.
What have these things to do with the human condition?
I am merely not blind to Ogden. I see now
What a fool Ogden has been all of these years,
And it is only now that our friendship can begin.

Enter OGDEN SIGAFOOS

REGINALD

Ogden! This is certainly a surprise!
We thought you were still in California.

OGDEN

I flew east today on my way to England,
And thought I might as well drop in to say goodbye.
Have you any more gin? It was hot in the plane.

REGINALD

There's plenty of gin, and...

ELSIE

But tell us, Ogden,
Whether you have seen Mildred? Mildred
Is in Cedar Rapids, Reginald says:
I suppose there may be a difference, though,
Between Cedar Rapids and California.
In school I was thought very good at geography,
But I am not the same person I was as a schoolgirl.
Have you seen Mildred, Ogden?

OGDEN

Yes.
I have seen Mildred. I saw her at the station

And drove out with her. She will be here shortly,
As soon as she has paid the taxi driver
And brought her luggage up to the house.
You must ask me no more questions. And you must
Promise that you will not ask *Mildred* any questions.

REGINALD

But that makes me feel like an utter fool, Ogden.
Why should I not ask Mildred any questions?

OGDEN

Because you *are* an utter fool, Reginald.
And because you have never faced up
To the Reginald whom you thought you saw this
      morning
Offering his chin to your razor in the mirror.
You must find the answer to this yourself.
I can only show you that there may *be* an answer.

ELSIE

Reginald has not read *The Cocktail Party,* Ogden,
But I have been wondering whether you have read it.

OGDEN

I have not only read it, Elsie, I have seen it!
Seeing and reading are two different things
And yet there is a sense in which they are only
Two faces of the same thing. I have read it.
You must not ask me when or under what conditions.
And now I must go. My plane for England
Leaves New York in the morning. I have much to do.

MAXWELL

What will you do in England, Ogden?

OGDEN

If I told you, Maxwell, would you be better off?
Stick to your gin. It will not make you wiser
Than you are now. But it cannot make you less wise
And it may make you happier. That is as much
As people like you have to look forward to.

MAXWELL

Thank you, Ogden. I see what a fool I have been.
Go in peace, my friend,
And work out your salvation in diligence.

OGDEN

I think it a clue to your character, Maxwell,
That you did not leave these words for *me* to say.

Exit OGDEN

ELSIE

Now it is all quite clear. I know now
What it was that led me yesterday in town
To buy an Aleut dictionary, and a first-year reader.
I had thought it was simply my interest in languages.
Goodbye, Gregory. You seem very small to me now
And rather contemptible. But I forgive you.
Please send my things to my people in Albany.

Exit ELSIE

REGINALD

Good Lord! I never suspected anything
Between Elsie and Gregory! And what
Made Elsie leave like that? Could it be the gin?

CYNTHIA

No, it was not the gin, Reginald. But why

Should I attempt to make *you* see these things?
It will be a long road. And Aleut is not easy.
I do not think we will see Elsie again.

GREGORY

It was rather a shock at first, but I'm over it now.
I suppose she was having me on all the time,
But it *was* fun going around with her.
Though I always felt there was something strange
In the way she looked when I discussed novels.
I daresay I will never amount to very much,
But I think that tomorrow I will go to Scranton
And take the job they have offered me there.
Goodbye all.

ALL

Goodbye, Gregory.

Exit GREGORY

REGINALD

Well, it beats me! But let's have a drink to...

CYNTHIA

Of course it beats you, Reginald. What does not
Beat you? When have you not been beaten?
Although people like you do not always know
That being beaten is what is happening to them.
Some brandy, please. And don't spare the gin!
A little more than that, I should imagine!
If you have any minor weakness, Reginald,
It is a tendency to stop pouring too soon.
And now I will follow Ogden to the station.
I know, of course, that he will simply offer me
The chance to go on putting up with Maxwell.
You have always been weak, Maxwell, but I am used
        to you,

And so I am sure that I will go no farther with Ogden
Than to the station. I can find my way out.

Exit CYNTHIA

MAXWELL

I think, Reginald, that I must be going too:
I see that Cynthia forgot her teeth after all,
And I think I can catch her and Ogden at the station.
Cynthia is always lost without her teeth,
Though I can't say they really improve her appearance.
May I take a bottle of your excellent gin?

REGINALD

Of course, Maxwell. But...

MAXWELL

Goodbye, Reginald.
I will leave by the back door if you do not mind.
I would rather not meet Mildred. Do not ask
My reasons, but give me the gin and I will go.
Do not force Mildred to explain anything:
For people like you and Mildred explanations
Explain nothing that could not have been explained
Without the explanations in the first place.
Goodbye, Reginald.

REGINALD

Goodbye, Maxwell.

*Exit MAXWELL. Alone, REGINALD kicks over a fragile table,
which crashes with its burden of glasses and bottles. Enter
MILDRED.*

MILDRED

What in the world was the matter with Ogden

And with all the others? They hardly spoke
As I passed them by coming up the walk,
But only smiled the *blandest* sort of smiles
And hurried on. Did you insult them, Reginald?
What have you been up to? Are you drunk again?

REGINALD

Why, my dear...

MILDRED

And what did your telegram mean?

REGINALD

Telegram? What telegram, Mildred?
I didn't send you any telegram.
Why in the world *should* I send you a telegram?
I was planning to write you a letter tonight,
But I certainly did not send you a telegram.

MILDRED

It was signed "You Know Who." I naturally assumed
You were probably drunk and trying to be funny.
But it did allude in a very odd way
To Elsie Diefenderfer. What *about* Elsie?
Don't tell me you've become *that* big a fool!

REGINALD

Elsie? Good God! But as far as that goes,
What about *Maxwell?* He hinted at something
Just as he was leaving. I thought he was tight.

MILDRED

If that is a joke, I think it's a poor one!
You know I have always thought Maxwell a creep,

89

To use an expression *you* might understand!
Well, I'm home anyhow. And I am not surprised
To see you have made your usual mess.

REGINALD

There is one thing, Mildred, I would like to know
Before we get back to quarrelling again,
And that is—have *you* read *The Cocktail Party?*

MILDRED

The Cocktail Party? Of course not! What *is* it?
And what a time to bring up literature!
You *are* drunk, Reginald! The house reeks of gin!
What a question to ask! You know perfectly well
That I have very little time for reading!
If it is one of those things that the men in your office
Have copies made of for private circulation
I don't want to hear it mentioned again!

*REGINALD looks at MILDRED for a moment, then moves to
embrace her. As she backs away, the UNIDENTIFIED CORPSE
suddenly rises from the sofa and, groaning, staggers from the
room.*

MILDRED

Dr. Cassidy! What was *he* doing here?

*Before REGINALD has time to answer, the CURTAIN abruptly
falls.*

1951

Interview with Ed Rasmussen

Furioso takes a twofold pride in bringing to its readers this interview with Ed Rasmussen. In the first place, of course, our pride is owing to the high position which his novels occupy in American literature. But more than this, perhaps, we feel—at a time when the world at large is moving ever closer to chaos— that we are at last meeting a public obligation which hitherto we have inexcusably neglected: every other important journal of opinion on this side of the Atlantic has long since published at least one interview with an author.[1] We hope herewith to make some small amends.

Our interview took place in the Ojibway Room of Al's Lounge and Grill in Minneapolis, where Mr. Rasmussen was briefly grounded during his recent flight to Winnipeg. The novelist was questioned by the entire staff of *Furioso,* but in the transcript no attempt has been made to name individual questioners, lest the more timid or less witty be put needlessly to shame.

It is hardly necessary to remind our readers that Ed Rasmussen was born in Teaneck, New Jersey, on St. Botolph's Day, 1898; that he has published more than thirteen novels; and that his first wife was Miss New Jersey of 1922.

* * *

F. Mr. Rasmussen?
R. What can I do for you?
F. You *are* Mr. Ed Rasmussen, the novelist, aren't you?
R. That's right.

---

1. The *New York Times,* for instance, has a man who seems to do little else than interview authors, and very competently, too. We only wish we had his knack.

F. Well, Mr. Rasmussen, I, we, hope you don't mind our "barging in" on you like this, but Al[2] told us he didn't think you would mind, and we certainly would appreciate it if you wouldn't mind telling us something about yourself. As a writer, that is. Of course, your private life...

R. What makes you think I want to tell you anything? A writer's supposed to *write,* not sit around saloons in Minneapolis or anywhere else telling people about how he writes or why he writes or *what* he writes. Hemingway simply refuses to talk about himself as a writer. Are you people from *Time?*

F. No, sir, we're from *Furioso.* Speaking of Hemingway, sir, what is your opinion of him? By that I mean, what do you think of him?

R. Oh, he had it, all right—*when* he had it. *Furioso?* What's that?

F. It's a quarterly magazine, sir. Kind of a literary quarterly, you might say. I wonder—that is, would you mind if we printed what you just said about Hemingway? We'd like to, if you wouldn't mind, sir.

R. Literary quarterly, eh? Never look at them. A writer's got no business reading literary quarterlies. *(Pause.)*

F. Yes, sir. But about Hemingway...

R. What about Hemingway?

F. About what you just said about him. I mean, having it *when* he had it. Could we publish that?

R. Sure, why not? Publish away. *(Pause.)*

F. Mr. Rasmussen—will you tell us something about your methods as a writer? How you go about it, that is?

R. You mean do I use a quill pen or a typewriter? *(Laughter.)*

F. Well, yes, sir, that too if you like. But what I meant was more your *methods.* I'm not sure I'm making myself clear, but...

R. That's all right, I don't mind getting you off that hook, son. How do I know what my methods are? A writer has no business worrying about such things. I might get an idea from almost anywhere—newspaper obituaries, an old seed catalog,

---

2. Al Chekhov, proprietor of Al's Lounge and Grill.

my grandmother's love letters, stuff I pick up in barrooms or zoos. It's up to the critics to find the symbolism. But don't get me started on *critics!*

F. No, sir. *(Pause.)* Well, sir, I wonder if you—that is, did you write *Put Up Your Bright Swords* that way? Or how did you, anyhow?

R. Why drag all that out in the open? As a matter of fact, the idea came to me while I was riding the Lehigh Valley rail-road from Buffalo to New York in October, 1934. I couldn't get any space on the New York Central that time, and the Lackawanna only goes to Hoboken, so I took the Lehigh. Right into Penn Station. There was this couple in the berth across the way, and around two-thirty a.m., well, this hor-rible laughing began.

F. Yes, sir?

R. That's it, more or less. After that the book pretty much wrote itself. The only point I was *conscious* of making had to do with man's indomitable courage in the face of hideous frustration. But I also wrote the book to make money, and it's always amused me to see how some of the critics strained to interpret Jocko's having an epileptic fit when Hilda and Larry crawl in the doghouse. Tennessee Williams sent me these clippings. Maybe there was one from this magazine of yours. What did you say you call it?

F. *Furioso,* sir. But do you mean, sir, that Jocko's being a pile-driver operator doesn't *mean* anything?

R. It means whatever you want it to mean, my boy. I just wanted to write a pile-driver into a novel, and that was my chance.

F. Oh. *(Pause.)* Well, not to change the subject, Mr. Rasmussen, because we all think *Put Up Your Bright Swords* is a great novel—I guess what I want to say is, how has living in New Jersey all your life affected you as a writer? If it *has,* that is.

F. How has it *affected* me? Of course it has! I don't mean I'm a member of the so-called New Jersey School, that kind of

93

labelling is idiotic, but how can you help being affected if you've lived in New Jersey all your life?

F. I always thought Jocko was a typical New Jersey type.

R. Right you are, young lady! I won't attempt to explain it in gaudy jargon, I leave that foolishness to the critics, but for me Jocko *is* New Jersey. And by "New Jersey" I don't mean Montclair or the Oranges or Princeton.

F. But didn't Larry go to Rutgers? As I remember, he did. Of course, I...

R. Sure Larry went to Rutgers. So what? Larry wasn't *Jocko*. Larry is no more New Jersey, the way *I* mean New Jersey, than you are, or than this young lady is Hilda. Hilda is *partly* New Jersey, and Jocko *sensed* that, in spite of the Bergdorf-Goodman bathrobe and the contact lenses. It's a long time since I wrote the book, and frankly I'd rather not talk about it, but one scene I do recall is the one where the pile-driver hits the old pre-Revolutionary-War water main *just* as Jocko sees Hilda riding by in her convertible for the first time. If you don't remember that scene, you simply don't remember the *book*.

F. *(Chorus of,* "I remember it," "Oh, sure," "Unforgettable!" "Certainly do, sir!" *etc.)*

R. I wonder if you do. You people are just like the American public in general these days, you've got all sorts of improved techniques for seeing things but you can't see them straight. Maybe you read too much. Maybe you read the wrong kind of stuff. Joyce had to face the same problem. *(Pause.)* I bet not one of you ever caught a seal with your bare hands.

F. *(Chorus of,* "No, sir," "A *seal?* with your bare *hands?"* *etc.)*

R. Well, I won't go into *that*. It's obvious you've never even looked at the dust-jacket to *The Cheek of Night*.

F. Oh, sir, I did look at it, all of us did, it was one of your best. We all thought when it came out that it was a *great* dust-jacket, Mr. Rasmussen. But I guess I personally was so fascinated by the account of how you let your beard grow when you were working on a book that I guess the seal. . .

R. God damn it, that's what they *always* remember! That god damned beard! Do people get obsessions about Hemingway's beard or Shakespeare's beard? The simple fact is, when I write I *can't* shave. Didn't you ever hear of Samson? Not to keep harping on my own work, but why did you suppose I made Jocko give in to that impulse to stop at the barber shop on his way to that last meeting with Hilda? Sure, I had a lot of notes for a barber shop scene—but that wasn't all. I imagine you've forgotten that too, eh?—or maybe, like everybody else, you got all wrapped up in that flashback about the manicurist and the corpse.

F *(Chorus of,* "Oh, no, sir!" "It's a wonderful scene," *etc.)*

R. I must have had a thousand letters about that flashback to every *one* about Jocko stopping for a shave and a haircut.

F. But it was a great flashback, Mr. Rasmussen.

R. That's not the point.

F. No, sir. *(Pause.)* Uh, speaking of *The Cheek of Night,* as we were, sir, a little while ago—I've always wondered if you modelled Buggsy on Dos Passos. I remember some of the critics—but you don't have to answer that, if. . .

R. I don't mind answering it. No. That is, not intentionally. I never consciously model my characters on actual people. I know a lot of readers thought Buggsy was Dos Passos, but a lot also thought Ike in *Back Blast* was Truman Capote. You'd be surprised at the number of angry letters I got from Capote fans. The truth is, the first time I ever met Capote was about six months after *Back Blast* was published, in a little dive in the Village. Capote was there taking notes and I was there taking notes and we happened to have adjoining tables. Since we were the only people in the place taking notes we naturally got to talking about them, and that was the first time we met.

F. Gee, we're certainly glad to know that, sir. *(Pause.)* That is, I know *I* am, and I'm pretty sure the rest of us are. *(Pause.)* But speaking of Dos Passos and Capote, sir, would you mind telling us how you rate American writers? Of the present day, that is.

R. That's silly. What does rating writers prove? What kind of magazine did you say you're from?

F. Why, it's sort of a literary quarterly, sir.

R. I thought so. Well, obviously you can't have any list without Hemingway and Faulkner. They both had it, *when* they had it. Dos Passos? Wolfe? Steinbeck? O'Hara? Sure, maybe. Then there are some of the younger crowd who might pan out. But I don't read novels any more. Hardly ever.

F. Thanks a lot, sir. But I think you left out your own name. . .

R. Did I? Well, if we have to, let's put it this way—if Hemingway in his prime had written *Back Blast* where would *The Sun Also Rises* rate now? Not that it wouldn't *rate,* mind you. But *where?*

F. Gosh, I never quite thought of it that. . .

R. I could be biased, of course; *Back Blast* is the book of mine that I like best. Now I suppose you're going to ask me, "Why?" That's usually the next foolish question. "Why?" How do I know why? All I know is, *Back Blast* felt *right* while I was working on it. The funny thing is—I'm not sure I ever told anyone this before—it started out to be a short story. But when Nancy killed her sister's pet rooster, I knew I had to go on—something was driving me. Maybe you'd call it the finger of God, but what*ever* it was, it was *there!* The book practically wrote itself, once I got past the scene where the sister tells Nancy's lover about the rooster. That was tough—almost as tough as the scene in *Put Up Your Bright Swords* after Larry sees Hilda running the pile driver, when he has to go out on the picket line as if nothing were bothering him but the state troopers' machine guns.

F. Gosh, Mr. Rasmussen, it certainly is interesting to hear all this! *(Chorus of,* "You bet it is!" "Gee!" "If I ever *did* know that, I'd completely forgotten it," *etc.)* Sir, we don't want to take up too much of your time, but we still have a couple of—that is, could you tell us a little about the book

96

you're working on now? What I mean is, I saw a story in *Newsweek,* I think it was, about a month ago. Maybe it was *Time.*

R. Look—when you people came in here, I told you a writer has no business talking about his own stuff. Leave that to the critics. *His* job is *writing.* Well, that goes double for a book he's still working on. *(Pause.)* You know where *Newsweek* got that information?

F. No, sir, I don't believe I. . .

R. From the janitor of a place where I used to live in Jersey City. He hated me for putting old typewriter ribbons in the trash can. Said they got his hands dirty. Imagine that?

F. Some janitor! *(Laughter.)*

R. Of course, *Newsweek* couldn't help getting *some* of it right. For instance, a few of the characters from *Put Up Your Bright Swords* are in the new book, and Hilda *does* have a vision of Saint Rose of Lima while she, Hilda that is, is kneeling beside Tom's body in the auto graveyard in Trenton. But *Gladys* is going to be the Mother Superior in the epilogue, not *Hilda.* Hilda will be discovering that the peace of God doesn't come cheap—that's why I'll have her struggling with first-year Latin grammar while the other nuns are walking in the cloister after vespers. And it's Ned, *not* Larry, who's going to capture the Omsk radio station after that parachute jump. While *that's* going on, *Larry* will be in the cardinal's study confessing the murder of Tom. But the mysterious monk who walks to the electric chair with Larry *is* going to be Jocko. They got *that* right, anyhow.

F. I certainly hope you're going to let us print all this, Mr. Rasmussen. I'm sure our readers. . .

R. Go right ahead and print it, if you think it'll do any good. This whole business is crazy, this interview I mean, but then the whole world is crazy as far as that goes.

F. I don't mean to interrupt, sir, but would you mind telling us what this new book is going to be called? The title, that is.

R. "Called"? How do I know what it's going to be called? That problem can wait. I suppose your next question will be how long does it take me to write a novel.

F. Why, as a matter of fact, sir. . .

R. How can anyone say how long it takes to write a novel? Three months, five months, two years. Balzac spent eight years writing *The Red and the Black.*

F. But, Mr. Rasmussen. . .

R. Maybe it will take me a month. Maybe sixteen months, like *The Cheek of Night.* Some days go faster than others, that's all. I begin writing about eight o'clock and knock off at three. Never eat lunch. Then at three-thirty I have some rye and ginger ale and a turkey sandwich. If the weather's decent I may get in a few sets of tennis. . .

F. But, sir, Balzac didn't. . .

R. In the fall I usually manage to do some hunting. Rabbits, mostly, around my part of Jersey, but they give you a run for your money. Evenings I read—Thackeray, Proust, Dostoevski, Balzac. You can't go wrong on them—they *had* it. What it takes. You ought to spend more time on them and less on this interviewing.

F. Yes, sir. *(Pause.)* Well, sir, we're certainly grateful to you for all you've been telling us, and for taking this time. *(Chorus of,* "We certainly are!" "Gee, wasn't that interesting?" *etc.)* But if you don't mind, sir, there's one last question. If you don't mind, that is.

R. All right, let's have it.

F. Well, it's sort of hard to phrase it, sir—but do you have any advice for young writers? I mean writers who are just starting out. To write, that is. Not that *we're* exactly *young,* but some of our readers. . .

R. Advice? Hell, no! A writer's got no business giving advice. A young writer should spend his time *writing,* not *talking* about writing. Writing all the time, about everything. It's up to the individual, of course, whether to keep a notebook or not, but it helps—*I* buy these little notebooks at

Woolworth's for a nickel, you don't need anything special. Did you know that Proust kept notes on paper napkins, to deaden the sound? The important thing is, *write! write! write!* If you want to be a writer, you've simply got to *write!*

F. Gosh, sir, thanks an awful lot! *(Pause.)* And now I guess we'll let you go. *(Laughter.)* You've been very good, that is, patient and helpful, this really ought to—anyhow, I, we, certainly hope you'll have a pleasant trip to Winnipeg. *(Chorus of,* "We certainly do!" "Winnipeg's a beautiful old city," *etc.)*

R. Think nothing of it. Anything you've managed to pry out of me, you're free to use. Of course, the trip to Winnipeg is nothing I care to go into detail about, but if any of you happen to know the reredos in the Winnipeg cathedral, well, don't be too surprised to find something like it turning up in the new book.

F. *(Chorus of,* "Gee!" "We'll certainly look for it, sir!" "I hear it's a wonderful reredos," *etc.)*

R. And don't forget to send me a copy of this magazine of yours when it comes out. *Furioso.* Got it right that time, didn't I?

F. Yes, sir. It's sort of a hard name. . .

R. Before you leave—how many of you people remembered that Hilda's grandmother came from Winnipeg? *(Pause.)*

F. I'm awfully sorry, sir, but. . .

R. Well, it's no more than I expect. I don't mean to be personal, you're not the only ones who wouldn't remember. As I see it, that's the sort of thing a writer has got to get hardened to, in our kind of world. It almost killed Henry James.

F. James, sir? But James. . .

R. Anyhow, it was nice to have this little talk with you. But you cut out wasting your time on this interviewing and get busy with your own writing. If you write, that is.

F. Yes, sir, we certainly will. Not that we could ever hope to. . .

R. If you do write, the thing to do is *write*.

F. Yes, sir. *(Pause.)* Well, thanks again, Mr. Rasmussen. *(Pause.)*
    I guess we really have to be going now. *(Pause.)* Well, good-
    bye, sir. And thanks again.

R. Don't mention it. *(Exeunt interviewers.)*

1952

Some Notes on the Early History of the Term "Jazz"

(Summarized from *Cats on the Tiles*, N.Y., 1954, a study of jazz history by Clifford Coan, the Canadian musicologist.)

The old argument about the origin of the term "jazz" seems finally settled by Coan's researches into the Gullah music of the South Carolina coast. In the Gullah dialect "jass" is the word for "yes," and the oldest and most popular Gullah song (both a worksong and a playsong) makes much of the word:

1. No sin-a jass jass   Now sing yes yes
   No sin-a jass jass
   No sin-a jass jass
   No sin-a jass jass   (This stanza is repeated
                                  3 times)
2. Di lel shi sin-a jass   This little child sings yes
   Do lel shi sin-a jass   That little child, etc.
   Di lel shi sin-a jass jass
   Do lel shi sin-a jass jass
   No sin-a jass!

                                  (This stanza, repeated 3
                                  times, is followed by
                                  stanza one)

The Gullah accompanied these verses, which might be sung for hours on end, with handclapping, stomping, and (on special occasions) the "gitto," or 9-stringed Gullah guitar—"really more a sort of double-banjo than a guitar properly speaking" (Coan, p. 57). "No one who has not heard the Gullah, drawing in their fishnets or simply relaxing before a cabin fire, sing these simple words, with infinite subtle variations of cadence, can imagine their extraordinary richness when rightly performed" (Coan, p. 61).

The word "jass" was brought to New Orleans in the late

1880's or early 1890's by a young man of the Gullah "with the somewhat improbable name of Leonard Olsen, the rather more probable nickname of 'Fatback.' " (p. 62) "Fatback" went to work on the docks as a stevedore, and as he sang at his hoisting of bales of cotton or pods of tobacco, or after hours in the "pokeyhouses" or "bocabbos" (beaux cabarets) of old New Orleans, he became something of a legend, both for his physical strength and for his rendering of "No sin-a jass jass." One of the most famous fights in New Orleans history resulted from an attempt by another famous "dockwalloper" of the period, a huge man known simply as "O Big Jeff," to stop "Fatback's" singing. "The epic battle is said by P. I. Baldwin in his *Folkways of the Delta* to have lasted nearly five hours and to have ended with the utter defeat of 'O Big Jeff.' Apparently no one else ever dared try to silence 'Fatback's' tremendous baritone, which could—at least, so legend has it—be heard for nearly a mile over the noises of the docks" (Coan, pp. 68-9).

Other new Orleans musicians began—at first possibly as a joke—to add the Gullah lyrics to their repertory, so that "by the end of the 90's 'sin-a jass jass' had become a 'household word' in those equivocal purlieus where New Orleans music was taking shape" (Coan, p. 73). At some period still undetermined the terms "jass song" or "jass tune" and finally "jass" alone were transferred to the kind of music which was to become jazz. " 'Jazz' is, of course, to those familiar with the speech of the lower Mississippi Delta, an inevitable way of pronouncing 'jass' " (Coan, p. 75).

"Thus," writes Coan (in concluding his chapter, "Roots in the Gullah") "to an undeservedly obscure and even partly mythical folk-hero of nearly six decades ago the world owes a term which is probably better known internationally than any other word in any other language. The American teen-ager, the British 'spiv,' the French *gars*, the Japanese *hakigako*, the Russian *malchik*, the Burmese *u-faw*, even the Tahitian *po-i-tahomi* might 'flunk' a question on, say, 'realpolitik' or the proton. But they would know 'jazz'—every one of them. It is high time that we do fitting honor to the memory of 'Fatback' Olsen!" (Coan, p. 78)

(It may be appropriate here to mention that Clifford Coan is presently—December,1954—engaged in organizing a jazz festival in honor of "Fatback," to be held in Ottawa in July, 1955, under the auspices of Jazz-North, the most important Canadian group of the kind. In a recent letter to the author of these notes "Cliff" Coan wrote, "We are hoping to make the Fatback Festival the best thing of the sort ever attempted—both a survey of the whole history of jazz and a sort of rallying-point—excuse the stuffy language—for the people in the States and here who are really serious about this kind of music. Naturally our plans are still pretty much up in the air, but we are pretty sure of a young Gullah lad who we think can sing 'No sin-a jass jass' the way Fatback himself would have done it. He's shy and he's scared about leaving home—God knows what idea he has of Canada— so we're keeping our fingers crossed. I'm going to Florida in January and will stop off to talk to the lad and his family and I hope get things definitely settled. . . You can't imagine the enthusiasm this project has stirred up hereabouts. Anything you can do for us we'll very much appreciate. Glad you like the book, especially the Gullah chapter. I've had some nasty letters about it, also some very nice ones, but I'm sticking to my guns.")

1954

103

A Minor Elizabethan

The following passage is from Professor Giovanii Cavallo's *Storia del Dramma Inglese (History of English Drama)*, Turin, 1937; translated (1953) by Dr. Bernard Mosher; chapter 7, pages 118 ff.

****

[Cavallo has been suggesting that sometimes an age may be more clearly seen through its minor than its major figures. He continues:]

And so, with this in mind, let us consider the career of a strikingly minor Elizabethan—that little-known adventurer, translator, poet, and hanger-on of great men, Christopher Pilchard, of whom the late Professor Grimes of Cambridge wrote in 1913, "Surely, few men of his age could have been more entirely Elizabethan."

Born in 1558, the year of Elizabeth's accession, Pilchard lived a long and extremely disordered life, and died the year of the closing of the theatres, of which we said something in the last chapter. Scion of an ancient Kentish family (his great-uncle, Sir Nicholas Pilchard, was said to have introduced Anne Boleyn to Henry VIII), Christopher was the godson of Thomas Sackville, who is reported to have observed of him, "The lad may conquer the world, an [if] Fortune do not let [prevent] him." A brilliant scholar, as his time regarded scholarship, the youthful Pilchard might have looked forward to a great career in church or state, had not an incorrigibly wild spirit caused his dismissal from Cambridge in 1575 for incessant brawling and dicing. Two madcap years in London followed; then he sailed with Drake in 1577 on what would turn out to be the famous circumnavigation of the globe.

His career for some years after his return to England from this voyage is not entirely clear, although he is no doubt the "Kit Pilchard Gent," who translated Ovid's *Amores* into "Englische baudie" in 1583, and he seems to have made acquaintances at court and to have had a hand in a masque or two. That he gave Inigo Jones that artist's first drawing-lessons, as he claimed to have done, is very doubtful: as we shall see, Pilchard was given to such extravagant and unlikely assertions. In any event, he turned his boundless energies towards the theatre (perhaps after service against the Spanish Armada), and in the late 1580's was on more-or-less good terms with Kyd, Marlowe, Ford and others of that famous early generation of popular playwrights. It would appear that he did some acting, and he could have created the role of Balthasar; certainly we cannot be as sure of his style of acting as we can be of that of more famous players of his day. A letter of Burbage's indicates that he was seriously injured, perhaps permanently crippled, in a fight in The Theatre with certain fellow actors, and apparently he never trod the boards again—a fact at which the other players "mightily rejoyced," according to Jonson as quoted by Drummond.

Involved in serious charges of smuggling Flemish lace into England, Pilchard escaped to Holland disguised as a Dutch parson, and for some years in exile on the continent arranged engagements for troupes of travelling English actors. Was it he in these years who suggested to Dekker the idea for Sir Giles Overreach? We cannot say, of course. We do know that in the early years of the seventeenth century Pilchard—by now "a middle-aged rascal," in Professor Grimes' phrase—was once more in England, somehow cleared of the charges of smuggling (he was singularly fortunate in his many scrapes with the law), and once more hanging about the theatres. There are references to him in Henslowe. Whether he killed a fellow-poet (Anthony Duckett) in a quarrel over an actress at the Fortune is more disputable. Dekker, in a pamphlet, called him "the vilest rogue of the age." Did he—as he characteristically asserted—collaborate with Beaumont and Fletcher? Was it in allusion to this that he named his only daughter Evadne? But such a claim is probably no less absurd than his later claims (made in extreme old age to his grandson, Thomas Pilchard, the notorious hanging judge of Derbyshire) that he had been the model for Wendell and had helped Webster polish the death scene of the Duchess. There is little room for doubt that he was the "C. Pylchyard" whom Ben Jonson thrashed in a brawl at the Mermaid Tavern for asserting that Jonson had stolen from him the theory of humours.

[Cavallo then goes on to an account of Pilchard's association with other poets and players, his further troubles with the authorities, his two marriages, his whirlwind affair when close to 70 with a lady-in-waiting of the Caroline court, and other matters.]

Of Pilchard's own dramatic work we have only the fragments of two tragedies, and one act of a play which he might have written, as he insisted he had, at the vigorous urging of Shakespeare. Despite a stirring as well as surprising defense of the conventions of the public stage, he seems in his own practice to have been rather faithful to Senecan and classic form . . . His qualities as a poet can be studied in what is perhaps the most famous single passage in his fragments, that in which the young Duke Cassino has just discovered, lying in "a foule ditche," the body of his mistress Delia, murdered at the command of their mutual friend and cousin, Beraldo, Count of Lombardy, who had been thwarted in his hopes of marrying her and thus gaining possession of her vast estates in the Pontine Marshes:

> What sight is this I see? My best belov'd
> And cherish'd Delia, jewell of this age
> And thread of gold i' the fabrick o' the world,
> In whom all sweetness and all joy were blent,
> 5   Strangl'd and quarter'd like a wretched beast
> And by a callous butcher hung in view,
> Her heart pluck'd forth, her very tongue cut out
> That once did make the summer aire rejoyce
> With concord sweet, her lockes befoul'd with bloude—
> 10   These lockes that erst these hands were wont to stroke,
> Softer than velvet and like honey sweet—
> As if the very starres were pull'd from heav'n
> And mired i' the filth of envious men;
> Her eyes, those lamps of grace, now cold and blanke

106

15 So that the oyster's selfe doth looke less dead
That fishermen are wont to drag from mud
That lieth 'neath the ocean's massy heaving
Near rocky coasts of distant Brittany!
Those eyes that oft on many a moonless night
20 Brought light and joy to cheerless Lombardy.
I cry, bereft of words, O woe is me
T'have seen what I have seen, see what I see!
No more will I in fair Bologna dwell,
Nor will all Italy suffice for me,
25 Where murder jesteth i'the face of God
And Holy Church herself's a nursery
And schoole for fiends that mock our Saviour's woundes,
But hence I'll hie me to some colder clime
Where bloude too hot is yet too cool for crime,
30 And there assuming a more humble guise
I'll plot revenge for slaughter'd Delia's eyes!

1958

107

(*L'Express,* 29 Février 1961.)

Cinéma

Le Nouvel Hôtel de "Bourgogne"

Armand Salaudcru pose quelques questions
à M. Norman-Davidov

C'est M. Norman-Davidov lui-même, habillé en bonze tibétain et coiffé d'une perruque Louis XIV ("pour mieux éviter les rhumes"), qui me reçoit à la porte de son appartement de la rue de Bourgogne. J'adore Paris, me dit-il, en prenant mon imperméable et mon chapeau. J'adore Paris, et c'est pour ça que j'espère que le jour viendra où Paris m'adorera à mon tour. Ou bien à son tour. Mon tour son tour? Je m'en f... pas mal! a ajouté d'une voix pétillante d'amour de Paris ce "Yankee" costaud, cossu, cosmopolite, aux lunettes de soleil quelque peu marcelachardiques, et qui du reste parle un français admirable, parsemé d'expressions argotiques que dans le quartier on trouve "d'un piquant! "

Et quand M. Norman-Davidov s'est-il mis en tête de venir s'établir à Paris et de tourner au cœur même du noble faubourg les petits films que notre cher maître et collègue, François Mauriac, a qualifié tout récemment dans son Bloc-Notes de "délicieusement canailles"?

Je ne saurais vraiment vous préciser, Monsieur, la date qu'a commencé mon adoration de Paris. Mais je suis convaincu qu'au moment même de mon entrée dans le monde j'aimais déjà Paris, et que j'avais déjà pris le parti de m'y installer définitivement.

Que les petits Américains en naissant songent déjà à habiter Paris, voilà une idée ravissante et qui ferait certainement plaisir à nos ancêtres les Gaulois. Et le cinéma?

Tout jeune j'habitais la Californie. Le cinéma était partout dans l'air, là où ne se trouve à présent que du "smog" Ou dirait-on plutôt "de la smog"? En tout cas, j'ai fait mes études universitaires à l'ombre même de Hollywood. Par la fenêtre étroite et sale de ma chambre d'étudiant je pouvais, en relevant ma tête de mon livre de Kant ou de Comptabilité, contempler l'énorme faux-ciel bleu du "back lot" (de "la back lot"?) de la Compagnie Twentieth-Century Fox. Ça m'a donné des idées!

Et la troupe de la rue de Bourgogne? Car je suis d'avis, M. Norman-Davidov, que les Comédiens Ordinaires du Roi qui jouaient il y a trois siècles rue Mauconseil au théâtre déjà un peu vétuste à cette époque qu'avait fait construire la Confrérie de la Passion vers le milieu du 16e siècle sur l'emplacement de l'ancien Hôtel de Bourgogne seraient rudement étonnés si par suite de quelque miracle peu souhaitable ils se trouvaient confrontés avec la troupe que de nos jours et dans un Paris tellement différent vous venez d'installer ici rue de Bourgogne!

Oui, d'accord, quoique ça serait assez amusant de recevoir chez nous des types comme Montfleury, Floridor, la Champmeslé! Mais notre troupe n'est qu'une toute petite troupe. Réponse modeste, et digne de cet homme modeste, mais qui ne cache tout à fait pas une fierté palpitante. Chez nous on aime mieux la qualité que la quantité! Ma femme et moi sommes convaincus qu'avec Mademoiselle Kiki, Mademoiselle Gogo, et Jean-Paul Pleurnichon, on a tout le nécessaire. Avec ces trois personnes quelque peu délabrées, peut-être, mais d'un talent incontestable, on peut merveilleuse-ment bien se débrouiller!

Et la vedette de la troupe?

Je dois vous faire remarquer, M. Salaudcru, que chez nous ne se trouve vraiment pas de vedette! Dans tel film c'est Mlle. Kiki qui prend le dessus, dans tel autre c'est Mlle. Gogo, dans un troisième c'est ce brave Jean-Paul. On tourne, pour ainsi dire, en famille—une famille dont les enfants sont tous gâtés!

Cela ne vous gênerait pas, Maître, de me dire les titres de vos films préférés? C'est à dire, bien entendu, des films que vous avez vous-même tournés!

Ah, zut! vous me posez là une question passionante mais bougrement compliquée! Et M. Norman-Davidov accompagne ce propos d'un petit clin d'oeil nerveux, en ôtant ses grosses lunettes de soleil, dont il mordille pen-dant quelques instants les verres. Eh bien—si vous tenez absolument à ce que je vous réponde, alors, je préfère *Fun at Fontainebleau, La Petite Vicieuse de Versailles, Les Caprices de Capri, L'Impromptu de Pigalle, La Belle Im-monde de Mons, Les Éboueurs de Bourges,* et *Les Précieuses Plus Ridicules que Ça.* C'est, du reste, tout ce qu'on a tourné jusqu'ici!

Alors, vous les préférez tous?

Indubitablement!

Il paraît que la géographie joue un rôle très important dans vos films. Ce sont plutôt des "travelogues"?

Ah, m...! et par exemple! Et M. Norman-Davidov d'esclaffer, en se grattant l'aisselle gauche avec son petit-doigt également gauche, ce qui n'est pas chose facile. Un gros rire américain qui fait trembler les lustres en cristal, les carreaux, le plafond, le plancher, les radiateurs, la vaisselle à la cuisine, la collection de pipes chinoises et de narguilés, le téléphone, les bibelots de toute espèce, le portrait peu flatteur de Mme Norman-Davidov par De Conninque, jusqu'à la perruque Louis XIV, jusqu'aux lunettes de soleil et aux boutons dorés du costume de bonze tibétain. Mais quelle idée bizarre! Est-ce que j'ai l'air tellement c..? Quoi! vous me prenez pour Tintin? Des "travelogues"?! Je vous assure, mon cher collègue, que chez nous on se f... de la géographie! On est classique! C'est à dire qu'on a remplacé le palais à volonté racinien par la chambre meublée à volonté moderne. On y met, sur la cheminée et afin de créer un peu de couleur locale très discrète, une photo de Fontainebleau, une vue aérienne de Mons, un portrait de Bismarck. Mais du naturalisme imbécile et démodé, on s'en f...!

Et Mme Norman-Davidov est tout à fait d'accord?

Tout à fait! À propos, je regrette beaucoup l'absence de ma femme, qui a été obligée de sortir ce matin de très bonne heure. C'est à cause de notre adorable Mlle. Gogo, qui a f.... le camp il y a trois jours; on a besoin d'elle, demain on va tourner *L'Ecole des Femmes,* après-demain *Les Femmes Savantes.* Toujours du Molière, un peu modifié. Ma femme cherche Gogo du côté de Belleville, c'est là bas qu'on la "découverte," et de temps en temps la nostalgie du coin la prend. Ma femme va être navrée à son retour d'apprendre qu'elle n'était pas là pour vous recevoir!

Voulez-vous bien m'expliquer ce nom "Normarj"? Je vous avoue, Maître, que je ne suis pas vraiment fort en anglais, et pour moi ce nom reste un mystère. Encore M. Norman-Davidov de rire ce gros rire du "far-West."

En effet, le mystère n'est pas tellement mystérieux! C'est un nom composé de la première syllabe de mon prénom et de la première syllabe du prénom de ma femme. Norman, c'est moi; Mar-jorie, c'est Madame.

Ah! bon.

C'est moi qui l'ai inventé, avec, bien entendu, le concours indispensable de ma femme.

Et vous êtes président de la compagnie "Normarj"?

Oui. Et le vice-président.

Et Madame Norman-Davidov?

Elle est secrétaire et trésorière.

Est-ce qu'il arrive quelquefois des histoires?

Une fois seulement! Le président a proposé à Mlle. Kiki d'aller passer ensemble un week-end à Boulogne-sur-Mer. Le vice-président se trouvant un peu éméché a eu l'imprudence de parler de ce projet à la secrétaire, qui l'a communiqué sans delai à la trésorière. On a discuté, on a mis des obstacles, on a émis des menaces, enfin le projet a été abandonné. Après, tout le monde est allé tres paisiblement casser une crôute—ou plutôt une choucrôute (je plaisante)—chez Lipp.

Et vos idées, Maître, sur la crise au Congo?

Je me f... de la crise au Congo! Ici on est des artistes, on trouve dégueulasses les questions politiques! Lorsque je tourne un film, c'est pour moi le retour au premier jour du monde! Kiki et Gogo, c'est deux Eves, Jean-Paul est un Adam deux fois béni! Et la chambre meublée à volonté, c'est un peu le paradis terrestre. Et ça suffit!

Ah! bon. Et vos idées sur Orçon-Ouell-z?

Ne m'en parlez pas!

Et Marlong Brandeau?

De grâce, Monsieur!

Et Jean Usthon?

Assez, Monsieur! Voici votre chapeau et votre imperméable! La porte est par là!

C'était ainsi que j'ai quitté ce Californien avisé et génial, mais en même temps un peu brutal. De la rue de Bourgogne aux Champs-Elysées j'ai marché à pas rapides, sans faire attention d'ailleurs à la circulation folle, aux chers bruits de cet énorme Paris, car je réflechissais toujours aux propos frappants du président et du vice-président des Films Normarj. Et me voilà déjà en face du Drug Store des Champs-Elysées avant de remarquer que le chapeau et l'impérmeable si brusquement restitués par M. Norman-Davidov n'étaient pas les miens, qu'ils n'étaient même pas français, mais que ces hardes étranges et fortement rapées portaient une étiquette exotique: "Moe Pinsky, Gents Furnishings, Westwood, Cal."

1961

Fulbright Report

WEST KENILWORTH STATE COLLEGE

Department of English   **Douglas Memorial Hall**

December 14, 1964

Committee on International Exchange of Persons
Washington, D.C.

Dear Sirs:

Please excuse my delay in responding to your request. I have been "down" with blackwater fever since my return in August from Pago Pago, and hence too weak to hold a pen or pencil, not to mention a typewriter. Today, however, I feel a little better, and seize the occasion to tell you something about my Fulbright year in Pago Pago. (I must say here, not without some bitterness, that no one in this country prepared me for what I was to meet in Pago Pago—I was not even informed about the correct pronunciation of the name [Pango Pango]! Surely such information should be given to future Fulbright lecturers there.)

I frankly feel that the situation is none too promising for American studies in that part of the world, even though there are compensations for the visiting lecturer of which I shall have something to say later in these remarks. The English Department at the University of Pago Pago is composed of three British "remittance men" *(was* composed, rather, for one of them died last Spring in delirium tremens) of unquestionably low quality— at least literarily speaking. Vulgar limericks and decidedly confused passages from Shakespeare unsteadily shouted while drunk appeared to be their stock in trade, on and off the campus. I was sorry to observe the students found something attractive about

112

these "professors," and roared with laughter at their slightest sally—although I was soon to discover that Pago Pago undergraduates, as well as graduate students, roar with laughter on practically any occasion. I was finally permitted to give a course in American literature, after much confusion in the office of the Dean (who for some weeks after my arrival treated me with truculent suspiciousness as a "spy" from some remote unspecified "headquarters")—a course which I felt it might be interesting to inaugurate by reading to the students Whitman's "Song of Myself," not only for the beauty of many (if not all) of its lines, but because it sums up the American character as it is revealed across a whole spectrum of strident self-assertions. I had hardly finished the first line ("I sing myself and celebrate myself") on the first day of the course—which was attended, on that occasion, by virtually the entire student body of slightly more than 900—when everyone burst into prolonged shouts of laughter, and I was unable to proceed, although I tried. So it went on the second day, and the third; so it went every day for eight and a half months. I never got past that line, and my class rather than decreasing in size seemed to swell as time passed. When the academic year was finally over, Dr. Chester Lilly-o-lilly, chairman of the Chemistry Department, told me that people from other islands as far as forty miles away had got into the habit of rowing over to Pago Pago for my "lecture" and the ensuing "fun." (Perhaps I should add here that Dr. Lilly-o-lilly was brought to the United States some years ago to study public speaking at Drake University, but owing to a "slip up" in the State Department office responsible for him, found himself studying chemistry at South Dakota. He seemed to spend most of his time in Pago Pago, professionally speaking, seeking new ways of improving the potency of the coconut brandy on which most Pago Pago-ans are virtually weaned.)

Of course the Fulbright people on Pago Pago and the American consul (really one and the same) were no help at all. In their rare moments of relative sobriety they seemed only to encourage this jesting indifference to Whitman's great poem, and, by

113

extension, to American literature in general. I was quite sure that the "gentleman" in faded khaki battledress and ridiculous false red beard who now and then turned up for my "course" was in fact the consul himself, a ne'er-do-well, though of good family, from Yale.

As for the compensations to which I have alluded above, the weather was ideal during my stay, and the food, while rather bland and at times "over-ripe," to say the least, not really insupportable, especially if washed down with liberal applications of the coconut brandy. And it was not later than the first night of my stay in the Pago-Pago Hilton (where our heedless consulate had found me "digs" at a rate considerably beyond what I had been led to believe— could there have been a "rake-off"?) that while lying awake shortly past midnight, mentally arranging and re-arranging the syllabus for my "course" (how innocent I was!) I became aware of a strange presence in my bed! For a moment I was terrified, thoughts of serpents, bandycoots, wild pigs, and other noxious vermin racing through my troubled mind! Then a veritable burst of giggles revealed my mistake—this was no exotic beast, but that year's junior prom beauty queen come to welcome me, in the way Pago Pago knew best, on behalf of the entire student body—which was at that very moment noisily celebrating some university tradition on the campus beach. Her name was Sarah (the old missionaries had left their traces in "Christian" names if not otherwise), and that night passed agreeably enough, as did all the nights that followed. Laughed at by day, I was "cajoled" by night in ways which I am sure most professors of American studies would find it hard to credit, even those who have held Fulbrights in Berlin, Rio de Janeiro, or Port Said. I hasten to add that I do not blame my blackwater fever on these contacts with my charming co-eds, contacts precious to me as a conscientious American teacher.

All the same, library facilities were, frankly, rotten—not so much nonexistent as worse than that! American literature was represented by two mildewed volumes of Zane Grey, a particularly insufferable volume of Elsie Dinsmore, the 1914 catalogue

114

of the International Harvester Company, and—*mirabile dictu*—a single copy of *PMLA*, from which half the pages had been torn for God knows what low reasons. As for textbooks, any mention of them by me brought further scowls from the Dean, further laughter from the students in general, and further bursts of giggling from the young Sarahs in my nocturnal "seminars." My faith in progress and in the future was sorely strained at times!

Blackwater fever is not a pleasant thing to have, but my predecessor at Pago Pago came out of his year with the yaws—far worse, I think. So in a way I suppose I may count myself fortunate. Certainly it was an experience which I could hardly hope to duplicate.

Very   sincerely   yours,

Nathaniel H. Melville, Jr.

1964

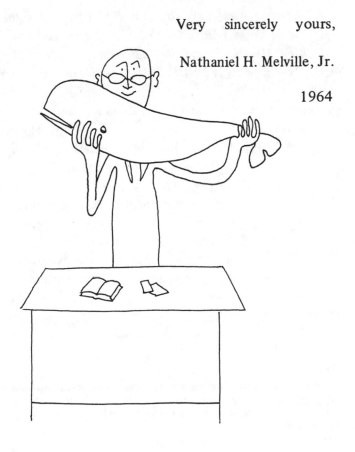

By Virtue Fall

Note:

Although Alvin Farquhar's play, *By Virtue Fall,*[1] is a fairly recent work (the late 1950's), the following account may make it sound old-fashioned to readers of 1965, their minds and hearts packed with Albee, Beckett, Ionesco, and Pinter—themselves already old-fashioned in this year of Le Roi Jones. And yet *By Virtue Fall* may strike such readers as strangely suggestive of these dramatists too, in spite of its happy or at any rate hopeful and (on the face of it) non-"absurd" ending. Can it be that the alienated modern consciousness knows no boundaries, that lost innocence repercusses everywhere, that (existentially *gesagt*) we are all in this thing together?

Some critics[2] have found in *By Virtue Fall* significant echoes of a little-known European play of many years ago—*Taking Up Slack (A Melodrama of the Classroom)*, the work (1911) of Bogdan Tomašević (1837-1931), Bosnian poet and man of letters, and one of that group of Balkan, semi-Balkan, and sub-Balkan geniuses who for so many decades labored in almost total obscurity to bring to their remote corners of the world the themes and forms of fiction and drama developed in the more "advanced" countries of northern and western Europe.

Bogdan Tomašević was by profession a schoolmaster who for more than seventy years drilled the rudiments of Old-Church Slavonic, business English, and commercial arithmetic into the minds—too often either rocklike or boglike—of the youth of Banjaluka. Yet he found time withal for an active life *extra muros,* so to speak—as a rapier-tongued wit in the popular Café de la Gare

---

1. Shakespeare's famous line is, "Some rise by sin, and some by virtue fall." Dr. Wallace W. Douglas used the first half of this line as the title of his sonnet sequence (1949-1953) on academic preferment.

2. Richard Ellmann, for one, in his essay, "The Unturned Stone," published in the volume *Fat Chance! / Essays, Studies, and Commemorative Verses / In Honor / of / A. H. N.* with original drawings by G[eorge] C[ohen], Evanston, Al's Maple Avenue Printshop, 1964. In his essay ("Why Wear a Truss?") in this same volume Professor Carl Condit digresses from his discussion of bridge-building to take sharp issue with Ellmann's argument.

(where for sixty-three years he occupied the same chair at the same table between the hours of 5:45 p.m. and 8:50 p.m.), and as a novelist and dramatist. From his fecund pen came some twenty-seven novels of Bosnian life and manners, and more than eighty plays—tragedies, melodramas, and comedies, many of them performed for the first—and, alas, only—time on the stage of the old State Theater of Banjaluka, a theater fated to be bombed flat in World War II. His biographer[3] tells us that Tomašević was, to the end, devoted not only to learning and letters but also to song, wine, and women in ascending order of importance: indeed in his eighty-ninth year the indignant parents of a Sarajevo high-school girl brought suit against him for contributing to the delinquency of a minor ("I didn't have to contribute much!" the aged wit retorted—then added with a twinkle, "Which is a lot better than not having much to contribute!")—a suit still pending in the courts at his untimely death from a surfeit of periwinkles in April, 1931.

While it is not impossible that Alvin Farquhar found some inspiration in *Taking Up Slack,* it is even less possible: Alvin Farquhar knows little Bosnian, and Tomašević's play has yet to be translated into English, although it appeared long since in German, Polish, and (curiously) Japanese. But even if the Bosnian bard *did* have some influence on the young American, *By Virtue Fall* is intensely American—"as American as Mom's anchovy pizza, or California sauterne," in the words of critic E[dmund] W[ilson] (?)—although these words were first applied to Melville's *Confidence Man* by Dr. Harrison Hayford in a Boston Atheneum lecture.

The account which follows of *By Virtue Fall* was originally presented in May, 1959, as a lecture at the meeting in Evanston, Illinois, of the National Association of Prison and County-Jail Librarians, with Dr. W. W. Douglas in the chair. It is published here with certain minor changes compelled or at least suggested

---

3. Radoslav Vukčić, the epic poet of Tuzla. His three-volume *Life* of Tomašević was published in 1934 at Trebinje, an event followed by several days of rioting by students.

by the passing of time, and by the fact that the play has in the meanwhile been performed with not entirely inconsiderable success both in the United States and abroad. Passages from the play are quoted by personal arrangement with the author's representative, Mrs. L. P. Nims of New York.

A word about the author: Alvin ("Peanuts") Farquhar was born on a soybean farm in Lancaster County, Pa., December 13, 1918, of wealthy Pennsylvania German parents. Educated in the local public schools, he received a B.S. degree in 1940 from Muhlenberg College, Allentown, Pa. He began to write fiction while employed as a timekeeper by the Gratz Tallow & Hides Co. of Emaus, Pa.—the family business of his first wife, Velma Gratz, Penn State '43. Discharged from this position in 1946 for reasons which have never been made entirely clear, Alvin Farquhar left his wife and two young children to seek his fortune in New York City, where he soon established valuable contacts with the tallow and hides interests of that place. Out of these experiences came his early novels—*Skin* (1947), *Cry Tallow!* (1949), *Anthrax* (1952), and *Hooves or Tails* (1955)—a "tetralogy" which according to Charles Poore in *The New York Times* "mingles a series of remarkably tangled yet touching love affairs with a mordant account, the most detailed we have yet had—in American fiction, at least—of the tallow and hides business. A *must!*"

Divorced from Velma Gratz in 1954, Alvin Farquhar took as his second bride, in May, 1955, the television actress, Tawny Plover. It was at her urging that he commenced writing plays— plays in which the attentive reader or listener may perhaps catch far-off echoes at times of such "giants" of our stage of yesteryear as O'Neill, Miller, Williams, and Macleish (or "Max Leash" as the poet is known in his favorite Broadway "show biz" haunts).

But enough, for the moment, of biography. Suffice it to say here that *By Virtue Fall* was composed during the summer and early autumn of 1958, and revised the next year.

* * *

118

There are a prologue and epilogue in verse, although Alvin Farquhar prefers the terms "Proem" and "Postlude." The Speaker in both is God, Whom the author, with an experimental daring that combines hints from William Blake and Tennessee Williams, calls Big Nobodaddy.

We never see Big Nobodaddy. He is always a Voice, a rich Voice from the wings or the flies. In the Proem Big Nobodaddy threatens, while in the Postlude he announces that he is not defeated by man, of course, but at least half persuaded of man's indomitable spirit. These lines are from the Proem:

Man—you think you've got My number,
But the truth is, I've got yours!
Shooting your mouth off's what you're best at,
But we'll see how you behave
When the chips're really down...

These lines are from the Postlude:

Man—you're luckier than you know!
Lucky but tough! I dig your style!
It's the style I really go for in
Shakespeare, Dante, and Macleish.

The play itself is in prose, the setting realistic (poetically so), the time a few years in the future, though not so many as to make the action impossibly fantastic. The place is a small community in southern Ohio, on the Ohio River. Here, among other tensions, north and south meet, struggle, and merge in moments of violence, passion, tenderness, grotesque humor, and terror, and of insights both Freudian and theological to which New York audiences responded with their usual flair for the equivocal, Chicago audiences with *their* usual ready laugh for any allusion to the bathroom.

The time of the action is from a Tuesday afternoon late in August (we are early made aware of an oppressive, exhausting heat) until noon the following day; like Pirandello (among others) Alvin Farquhar sees fit to compress his bold hunches into a rather conventional three-act form. The setting is the attic of a once grand and splendidly gingerbready but now seedy old Ohio

119

River-valley mansion, inhabited for generations by descendants of Jedediah Boom, a well-to-do river pirate hanged at Cincinnati in the middle 1840's. A stiff likeness of him in oils—apparently painted in the funeral parlor immediately following the hanging by some old-time journeyman portrait-painter—occupies a conspicuous place in the mounds of family treasures and random junk which clutter the attic—or *seem* to clutter it, for all is of course artfully arranged to achieve that poetry *of* the theater mentioned by Cocteau in a famous phrase. So we glimpse dusty old crinolines, stone jugs, broken birdcages (one of which contains a mummified linnet upside down on its perch), a wire dress form, crumbling files of *Harper's Weekly,* a mangy but dignified moosehead, a Civil War Union-foragemaster's uniform which Great Uncle Daniel Boom, the miser, saved to wear to the Spanish-American War as well; bones hidden here and there by long-vanished dogs; a symbolically shattered pier glass; a shiny old horsehair loveseat[4] on whose slippery surface many Booms have been precariously conceived, many family tragedies at last played out.

In this attic Mercy Boom, last child of the long line, and her husband, Lester ("Buck") Stork, have been living for some months when the curtain rises on Act I. The rest of the house, we soon learn, has been rented to construction workers on the new Ohio River dam, the completion of which will mean the flooding of the old Boom property and the end of an era in family, local, and national history. Now and then throughout the play, when the trap door into the attic is briefly opened, we hear the coarse shouting and horseplay of these workers, whom we may take, if we will, to stand for the mere brute in man. It is implied that they can never possibly understand the meaning of their dam-building, or what it will do to a lovely if somewhat faded way of life; or anything else, for that matter!

Mercy Boom is a ravaged beauty of rising two-hundred

---

4. Could Alvin Farquhar have been conveniently "remembering" such horsehair furniture from a notorious scene in one of Mary McCarthy's novels (either *Helbeck of Bannisdale* or *Sir George Tressady*)?

pounds, for her neurosis takes the form of compulsive eating. Indeed, some of the grotesque humor of the play, which critics have compared with Faulkner's [and more recently with Pinter's Ionesco's, Beckett's, and Albee's. (WBS, 1965)] has to do with Mercy's supposed gluttonous designs on the horsehair loveseat, although these designs have their serious implications too: *people like this are tragically self-consuming!* Her great sorrow, we learn with a *frisson* of pity and terror, is that her husband, "Buck" Stork shuns her. Very skillfully and with chilling suspense Alvin Farquhar leads his audience to the terrible secret of the haunted couple: "Buck" Stork is in love with the old wire dress form! Once we have learned this fact—guessed it, rather—we cannot keep our eyes off this object, as it looms, significantly-lighted, in the rat-infested ghost-ridden old attic.

A third character in this drama is Cousin Wally Boom, sixty years old, a member of the Bronx branch of the family. The reasons for his presence in the attic, other than to provide a note of petit-bourgeois tragedy and anguish, and therefore some contrast and variety, were not made particularly clear in the original script, or in the revisions.

The mute and skeletal dress-form is the source of bitter conflict between Mercy and "Buck," and the author is wise as well as skillful enough to make this conflict also involve by subtle implication present and past, north and south, east and west, the mythical and the meanly contemporary, love and hate, Europe and America, Henry James and Sinclair Lewis, a gracious former way of life and a mannerless modern one, Ezra Pound and Carl Sandburg, the body and the soul, *and* the ultimate wisdom of building across the Ohio River a dam which is certain to flood all southern Ohio and northern Kentucky, with an incalculable disruption of ancient folkways, and of much else besides.

Towards the end of Act I "Buck" emerges from under a pile of yellowed old lace fichus where he has been surreptitiously "consulting" with the contents of one of the antique stone jugs, and shouts his defiance of Big Nobodaddy:

121

BUCK

You—*you*—YOU—Y O U!—up there! Or out there! Or somewhere! You! Big Nobodaddy! *(Pause)* Think you're so all-fired
important, don't you? You *bully! (He hiccups with tragic intensity)* Put'm up and le's have a fair fight!

MERCY

Oh, Buck—please!—not again! Poor poor lost boy! For my sake,
Lester...

BUCK *(savagely interrupting)*

Don' you go call'n me "Lester"! Name's *Buck!* Drunk'r sober
name is Buck! What's *y'r* name? *(Suddenly mean)* Look at you!
Last faded bloom of the doomed Booms! *(His lips have always
puckered a little over this phrase; they do so now.)* Two hunnert
and thirty-five pounds! Of what? Of noth'n, tha's what! You—
you—cow elephant! *(He slaps her cruelly.)*

MERCY

Buck—dear dear haunted lost Buck, you mustn't ever do that!
It—it *hurts*! Or—if you must—*do* wash yo' hands first!

BUCK

Wash my hands? *Wash* my HANDS? Show me the water c'n wash
this dirt away! It goes right through, this dirt does! *(Raises his
hands)* You see them, Big Nobodaddy? Take a good look at'm!
You made them dirty! It's *your* dirt!

MERCY

Oh, Lester, Buck—my love, my darling! What's happened to you?

What happened to that charming boy that came co'tin' me in that old green Model A Ford with the red wheels and the mildewed buggy top and yo' dear mama in the rumble seat jus' *eatin'* yo' up with her eyes? What happened to the brave boy that knocked out the piano player at the high school senior prom with one punch 'cause he thought that ol' piano player said somethin' naughty to me? Only it wasn't that piano player at all, it was the tenor sax player. *(She giggles tenderly, reminiscing) His* name—the sax player's—le's see—his name was DuBose Lumpkin, that used to live in that big ol' lightnin'-struck house over on the hill and was such a beautiful dancer and went way up no'th to college and got himself plumb killed in that ol' *Ko*-rean war...

BUCK *(interrupting)*

Damn your cheap reminiscences, you—you—you she-hippopotamus! *(He points to the portrait of old Jedediah)* Look at *him*! Look at the old pirate! *He* knew how to live! What do *you* know? The old pirate's two-hunnert-and-thirty-five-pound if she's an ounce great great great grandaughter! Living in a dirty attic with the stuff the old pirate's dirty money built. Taking up half the space and most of the air!

MERCY

Buck, Buck, dearest heart. You're thinking of that—that—that *thing* again! *(She points to the wire dress form.)*

BUCK

Don't you dare mention it! You've got no right! Don't you ever mention it again, you—you—you girl-whale!

MERCY

I meant no harm, Buck. Only...

BUCK

Only what?

MERCY

Only. Well, forgive me, Buck—only I do think it a little bitty-bit strange when a grown man of thirty-six years falls in love with a dusty ol' wire dress form. It just don't seem *right* somehow! 'Course, maybe I'm foolishly readin' somethin' into it, but sometimes I lie awake at night and wonder how it happened. And then I begin to wonder what happened to *us*...

BUCK *(interrupting)*

You meant no harm! You—you—you female brontosaurus! You can't open your mouth without meaning harm! *(He collapses sobbing on the horsehair loveseat. Cousin Wally, waking from some long nostalgic dream of his own, speaks:)*

COUSIN WALLY

There, there, boy don't take on so!—Cousin Mercy didn't mean you no harm. She's just tryin' to help you, boy.

BUCK

Oh, shut up, you old goat!

COUSIN WALLY *(pathetically)*

Maybe you're right, boy. Maybe I am just an old goat, just an old lost and by the wind-grieved goat. *(Pause)* But I can tell you they was a time when I was a young goat! I'd go through all the cities of the north in that red Locomobile of mine and the entire population would set up and take notice! They knew me, boy, they

124

knew me. And they appreciated. Yes, boy, they appreciated. I never give less than a dollar tip to a shoeshine boy in my life. Many's the time the mayor of a town like Skeneateles, New York or Bradford, P-A, would come out to the city limits and insist on totin' my sample case right into town on their own shoulder. I was known, boy, widely known. Why, they was this waiter in the Hotel Cormorant in Hartford, Connecticut, that sent his oldest son right through the Yale University just on what he got from me in tips! And the graduate school too! 'Course he did come to find out too late that the boy had went into what they called the English department and didn't never amount to much. But that warn't the daddy's fault, no, nor mine neither! You can't blame parents for everything.

BUCK *(sourly)*

Bosh! [The stage nowadays permits a great freedom in this matter of expletives. For this reason, "Bosh!" may by now (1959) have, paradoxically, a greater shock effect than, say, *le mot de Cambronne* in its English form; or certain other "basic" words. Still, the actor is free to substitute his own favorite, if he must. (Alvin Farquhar's note) (I heartily subscribe. WBS, 1965)]

COUSIN WALLY

What'd you say, boy?

BUCK

I said "Bosh!"

COUSIN WALLY

That's what I figgered you said, and...

MERCY *(interrupting)*

Oh, Cousin Wally, don't pay no mind to that. Buck doesn't mean it. And Buck, dearest, try to not rile Cousin Wally up so! We've all got to get along in this attic and it's bad enough to have those vulgar men from the dam downstairs trampin' their mud all over mama's beautiful Brussels carpets and drinkin' beer and soda pop out of papa's Venetian-glass goblets without you two... Buck— just *look* at Cousin Wally! Can't you see what's happenin' to the man? Attention must be paid!

COUSIN WALLY *(lost, musing)*

Yes, sir, through all the cities of the north. I was known, well known, and widely appreciated. Places like Altoona, Pennsylvania; Bucyrus and Lima, Ohio; Dowagiac, Michigan; North Adams, Massachusetts; Blairstown, New Jersey—why, they'd practically roll out the red carpet right down the middle of the main street when they heard that I and that shiny Locomobile had hove into town!

BUCK *(cruelly)*

You never owned a Locomobile! You never owned *any* kind of a car!

MERCY

Buck, Buck, lover—please...

COUSIN WALLY

Never owned a car? Never owned a Locomobile? You tellin' *me* I never owned a car? Why, you—you—you—you young dress-dummy lover! You think I'm goin' to set here and listen to some young good-for-nothing imitation of a man that's moonin' around

126

after an old dress dummy tell me I dint own an automobile? I'd like to hear you tell that to the mayor of Scranton, P-A, that was mighty proud and honored to call me by my first name... *(Suddenly clutching his abdomen)* Oh—oh—that pain again!—that gas pain!

BUCK *(coldly)*

Gas pain! You're just *all* gas, old man! Just all gas!

* * *

But enough, for the moment, of this dialogue, at once so marvelously plain, yet so loaded with its own kind of poetry.

Act I soon ends, with the three doomed characters persistently hurting one another, each trapped in his or her own private agony, memories, despair. In Act II the bitter struggle continues, the old wire dress-form still the mute inglorious witness of all this human violence and hatefulness and sorrow. Then—just before midnight, and only a moment after Buck by a vast hysterical surge of strength has thrown Mercy in an airplane spin clear across the attic and full into the face of Cousin Wally—one of the construction workers pokes his head through the trap door to announce that the dam is now finished and the entire Ohio River valley on the point of being flooded. "You folks better git out of here while the gittin's good," he says coolly in an Italian or Polish or hillbilly (Appalachian migrant) accent, or any reasonable combination of the three. The second-act curtain descends on this revelation, as a sudden vagrant shaft of moonlight picks out the portrait of old Jedediah Boom while Mercy, "Buck," and Cousin Wally crouch stricken in the shadows.

How will it all work out? What decisions will these three make? What decisions *can* they make? Such are the questions with which the curtain of Act II has left us. It is in Act III that Alvin ("Peanuts") Farquhar proves himself a worthy candidate for that great roster which rolls from Aeschylus to O'Neill to Miller to Macleish [and beyond, to Ionesco, Beckett, Albee, Pinter

127

and LeRoi Jones. (WBS, 1965)]

At the opening of Act III the first reactions to the fatal announcement are desperate, directionless. Mercy, as custodian of the past, of family memories, rushes wildly about, picking up and discarding old possessions and heirlooms to be saved from the flood—rhinestone hatpins, old dance-cards, a sterling-silver ear-trumpet, an auburn "switch," antimacassars, serio-comic valentines. Distractedly, almost unselfconsciously, she slips into her long-dead papa's old white turtleneck sweater with the blue block-Y, and puts on her head the mantilla which Great Grandfather Lucius Boom, the family scamp, brought back from Madrid in the 1860's. At the same time "Buck," in pathetic pantomime, lovingly wraps the dress-form in his own T-shirt, with its stencilled University of Michigan wolverine still faintly visible on the front. Cousin Wally rages in violent, almost incoherent, quasi-Elizabethan rhetoric against a system which permits men and women to drown like rats and lose their homes for the sake of an unnecessary however fancy new dam, while the rats themselves are transported at the taxpayers' expense to safe new quarters on the high ground. From outside the house is heard a growing roar of rushing waters, and the *pétarade* of the outboard motor-boat hurrying the last construction workers to safety.

Then, suddenly, from the flies comes the richly resonant Voice of Big Nobodaddy:

MANY WATERS CANNOT QUENCH LOVE, NEITHER CAN THE FLOODS DROWN IT: IF A MAN WOULD GIVE ALL THE SUBSTANCE OF HIS HOUSE FOR LOVE, IT WOULD UTTERLY BE CONDEMNED.

For a moment the three characters are startled by this unexpected recitation from *The Song of Solomon.* For a moment longer they puzzle over the construction of the second "IT"—but no, that way madness, at the very least, lies. It is the word "LOVE" which has really seized them. Can this be some belated construction worker playing a prank from the roof? Hardly!—they know that Voice too well. And soon a change begins to set in.

"Love"? Here is a word not mentioned before—save in con-

128

nection with the dress form—in this grim struggle of egos, for even Mercy has been more devoted to admiring the sound of her own voice than to anything or anyone else. Will these sufferers permit Big Nobodaddy to shame them with His rather patronizing however apt citation from His Book? Can Big Nobodaddy respect *them* if they *do* let Him shame them thus? What *is* a man anyhow? Clearly, Man's indomitable spirit is at stake here, his will to survive, his courage to endure, his capacity for life and love and talking back to the boss—all those qualities which distinguish a man from a roach or a toad or a chicken or a cow, and which the critics invariably comment on in their reviews. It is a challenge to the characters, but a greater challenge to their creator, Alvin Farquhar. Unless he can get them out of this "fix" impressively enough, his work will hardly win the accolades which Atkinson [This was written in 1959. WBS], Kerr, and the rest reserve for masterpieces, or near-masterpieces: "brooding," "compassionate," "compassionately brooding," "deeply moving yet informed by flashes of rare humor," "compelling," "richly rewarding," and so on. [And what of the "highbrow" critics—Brustein, Bentley, *The Tulane Drama Review*?—where, by the way, a translation of Tomašević's *Taking Up Slack* is announced for imminent publication. Perhaps this will give us the answer we have been waiting for. (WBS, 1965)]

So it is that gradually, in dialogue at once convincingly true to life and dense with poetic implication, these three come to see themselves and each other, as well as their predicament (the *total* human predicament *in parvo*) with a clarity hitherto denied them by their own blind stubbornness and self-interest:

BUCK

"Love," eh? H-m-m-m- There's a word this old house hasn't heard for a long time—not to *mean* anything, that is.

COUSIN WALLY *(after a pause)*

Son, the commissioner of water works in Utica, New York, once

129

give me a definition of "love." What he said was, "Wally, boy, love is what makes the full pressure in the mains. Without which you just dry up." I always remembered that. *(Pause)* I used to set with him in his office in the Utica city hall and look out of the window watching all them people walking by on the sidewalk. *(Pause)*

BUCK *(with a new-found kindness)*

Well, Cousin Wally, I guess that's as good a definition as any, and better than some. I imagine all them—those—people in Utica appreciated too, when you went by in that shiny red Locomobile.

COUSIN WALLY

Well, sure. *(Pause)* Leastwise, I *guess* they did. *(Pause)* But not as much as I let on sometimes, boy. Fact o' the matter is, I stretched the truth a little bit here and there. That there Locomobile, f'r instance—well, it warn't exactly red. Or shiny. Shucks, I might as well tell you here and now, that Locomobile warn't really nothin' but an old Model-T Ford that dint even have an engine in it. I used to have to hire me a mule to tow it. *When* I had the price of a mule.

BUCK

If it was a Locomobile to you, Cousin Wally, it was a *Locomobile!* You go on clinging to that illusion! I can see now that illusions are about all that folks *have* to cling to. I only wish I had some! *(Pause)* I used to when I was a boy, but come time for me to leave home and go off to the University of Michigan, the first thing I saw when I hopped off that old bus in Ann Arbor was some members of the University of Michigan faculty walking by the bus depot. That sight fetched me up short right there, and I just never did seem to be able to work up any more illusions after that. I'd hate to have a son of mine go through that experience.

130

(Pause, then wistfully) If I *had* a son!

MERCY *(distractedly, the past surging up in her)*

What are we going to do, Lester? I can hear the river rising, rising, rising, rising, just like it used to do in flood time when I was a little girl in this house and mama would come in my room late at night in that white ball gown of hers that came all the way from Philadelphia, Pennsylvania, and take me in her arms and comfort me. She used to drink terribly at those times, but I got so I liked the smell of the whiskey or the gin or the wine or the brandy or the rum, or all of them sort of stirred up together. *(Pause)* Then papa would come in my room and belt her in the chops! That's what *he* used to say: "I'm going to belt her in the chops!" And he would! Even as a tiny child I thought that was a kind of funny way for a Yale man to talk. All the same, papa was a dashing figure in those days—six feet four in his uniform, a hundred and forty-five pounds—all lean muscle—and shoulders like he had a billiard cue under his jacket! And now...

BUCK *(interrupting)*

What are we going to *do*? I'll tell you what *I'm* going to do! Stay right *here* and fight this thing through! Show our friend Big Nobodaddy a thing or two! We can't go on living in the past!

COUSIN WALLY

Son, I don't like to sound timid or cowardly, because I got a score to settle with Big Nobodaddy too. But all the same, with the roof of the house under fifty feet of water it ain't going to be too comfortable stayin' on in this here attic.

BUCK

You think I'm going to be scared out by *that*? You can go if you

131

want to, Cousin Wally, and no hard feelings. And you too, Mercy. I'm staying!

MERCY *(after a pause)*

Ah, yes—I can see it all now. You want me to leave you with that —that—that dress form! Is that it?

BUCK *(after a pause, very softly)*

What dress form? *(Brief pause)* I don't see any dress form.

MERCY *(joyously)*

"What dress form?"? Did you say "What dress form?"? Oh, Lester, Lester! *(Pause)* I guess it's you poor, weak, beautiful, helpless, sick, confused, lovable people that win out in the end, after all! 'Cause you're really so strong! *(Pause)* If you stay, I stay! We'll show Big Nobodaddy! It's a whole new life starting over again. We can learn to make a new world of this old attic!

BUCK

It's not going to be easy, my dearest. We'll have to do without a lot of the luxuries we've grown accustomed to in our old world. Food. Air. Light. Maybe face chronic rheumatism and head colds. But just think—life itself on this planet began ages and ages ago in the wild waters of the world.

MERCY *(rapt)*

The wild wild waters! Just like Adam and Eve. *And* Uncle Wally. Dear Uncle Wally, will you stay too?

UNCLE WALLY *(after a pause)*

You *sold* me! And I reckon I'm just kinda used to you two

132

young-uns. Dampness or no dampness, I'm a-stayin'. Just try and get rid of me! I know it's a fool thing to do, but most things that ever got done that was *wuth* gettin' done was fool things to start with! *(He crosses to close the trap door in the attic floor, as "Buck" leads Mercy towards the old horsehair loveseat, which in the strange light seems suddenly transformed into a new horsehair loveseat. The stage is finally totally dark as)*

The Curtain Very Slowly Falls

[Here followed in the original lecture an account of the Postlude, which will be omitted here. Suffice it to say that with all its poetic magnificence, the Postlude seems a little dated in 1965. At last reports, Alvin Farquhar was hard at work on a new one, which will be "performed" in the television production of *By Virtue Fall,* now scheduled for some time in April (1965). Alvin Farquhar's wife, the actress Tawny Plover, is reportedly "building herself up" to play the role of Mercy in this production. We have much to be thankful for, after all. WBS]

1958, 1965

Vis'ting Fireman

(The following speeches are from Ben Jonson's very late and de-
servedly unremembered comedy, *The Olde Hat of Highgate*,
1634 (?). Here (I.iii.19ff) CHURLISH, the hero of the piece,
comments to SPAVIN, his friend and straight man, on the visiting PSEUDOMORPH.)

CHURLISH

Mark nowe your vis'ting fireman from abroade,
Your Allemain or Dutch closet theologian
Or French philosopher; or our fine Flemish poet,
His voyce as neatly rippl'd as his haire
5   That flowes like your cock-pheasant's curving taile
Athwart's poetic noggin; his jaw-bone too a weapon...

SPAVIN

(I warrant thee!

CHURLISH

       Nay, shut thy meddling chops.')
Regards the glist'ning phizzes of the young,
That gaze at him as donkeys at a fountaine
10   In a drye place, in fancy countes his profitts
(A tax he shareth on each youthfull poll),
Then not unhappy, having tot the score,
He reacheth in an oft-op'd old parcell
Of baubles, sleeke nugacities: shines, opines;
15   Or his tongue slices trenchers off his brayne
Like that machine which your Ital doth use
To cut his slablets of black rugose sausage,
Farcied with garlic, faugh! and wash'd with wine
Which these Chiant, those Orvieto call...

SPAVIN

20   And still will have his braine when all is slic'd!

CHURLISH

Right, yet must I ever pray thee, Hold thy maw!

Notes & Queries (by WBS)

(I must confess to a certain uneasiness about these lines, even though they offer clear evidence of what Gerald Epstein in *Dental News* called the "curiosa infelicitas" of Jonson's style (a playful yet admiring echo of Petronius' famous phrase about Horace). Perhaps these lines offer somewhat *too* clear evidence... h-m-m-m... yet.... Well!)

line

1. "vis'ting fireman" I have always taken this expression to be peculiarly American and modern! When did England first have firemen—and when did they begin "visiting"?

6. How are we to read the second half of this line?—"his jaw-bone *too* a weapon"? "*his* jaw-bone too a weapon"? The second way, I think, for its allusiveness; the first hardly makes sense in this context.

7. Such is the tone, throughout the play, of friendly exchanges between CHURLISH and SPAVIN; see line 21 below.

8. "phizzes" Is this really a "Jonson word"?

12. "tot" *Can* this be a legitmate variant of "totalled" or "totted"? Would even Jonson's linguistic daring have carried him this far—not to mention his desire to make the line scan right?

13. "Oft-op'd old parcell" Curiosa infelicitas or no, this does seem a bit over the mark! But the whole line is disturbing.

16. "Ital" (for "Italian") Again the poet seems to have taken undue liberties in order to make the line come out right; so with "Chiant" in line 19. Are such forms to be found in other works of Jonson, or in the works of his contemporaries.

16-17 Are we to believe that *machines* for slicing *meat* existed at this early date? To be sure, various ancestors of the guillotine had been in use for some time, but *sausage*! Yet we must avoid being too toploftily twentieth century, technologywise!

18-19 Jonson's well-known tendency (one he shared with his age) not to let well enough alone seems in evidence here. Yet would we sacrifice these lines in the interest of greater economy of means?

19. "Chiant" See note on line 16 above.

21. See note on line 7 above.

1965

Library Newsletter

A Prophet with Honor: George Cohen

Rarely has a Deering exhibit generated more excitement than the current "show" of canvases and "gummies" by N. U.'s very own George Cohen, crack painter of metaphysical anguish. In the words of Lancelot Costive *(Art News,* December 1964, 147-86), "George Cohen's recent *oeuvre* uncoils once again this artist's mastery of all those strategies by which the sonic boom is, so to speak, made flesh...."

Visitors entering Deering by the front door may almost immediately become aware of the large painting, "Variations on a Motif of Bouguereau" (42' by 67' 6"), which overhangs the lobby, and through which the lobby columns now thrust like bold jungle giants through low rain clouds on the Andean or Himalayan slope. Suspended face down from the ceiling, this picture compels the viewer to *look up,* if he would truly "see" it! Part of the *frisson* stirred by this extraordinary canvas is owing to the illusion that great blobs and globs of *wet paint* are about to fall *out of the canvas* and into the eye of the beholder (where beauty lies: Lancelot Costive writes feelingly of "the 'falling-out-of-the-painting-ness' of George Cohen").

On the second floor other paintings and "gummies" now take up the space ordinarily occupied by the card catalogue (temporarily banished to the Browsing Room), and by the Librarian—who has, in fact, been supplanted (not altogether disadvantageously) by George Cohen's monumental "gummy" of him ("Jensgummy No. 10"). (A "gummy" is, in the artist's own words, "a sculpture in masses of compacted chewing-gum, moulded, carved, pounded, slashed, shattered, stained, shellacked, as one chooses." For years the members of the Cohen family have been chewing gum "like people possessed" ["I don't know what it's done to our digestions," says Mrs George Cohen, "but we have jaws like piranhas!"] —placing the "finished" product in a gum-press constructed to George Cohen's specifications by master craftsmen of the Northwestern Department of Buildings and Grounds). In addition to the "gummy" of the Librarian ("260,000 sticks of Spearmint would be a conservative estimate," says George Cohen in answer to the obvious question), there are heroic "gummies" of Dean Simeon Leland, "the Ellmann family," Cantor Bernard Sahlins, Dr. Erich Heller, Counsellor Oppenheim, various Cohen pets, the Dean of Women, and "Connie" (Mrs Cohen). The numerous paintings include "Beach Rot" (26' by 14'), "Family Dentist" (really a "semi-gummy"), "Chinga ˌsu· Madre!" (a vaguely "Mexican," vaguely "devotional" canvas, its title from a ballad by south-of-the-border bard Robusto Cojones); "Uncle Roscoe" (wet ashes on casually-varnished sackcloth); " 'Look Out!' No 8" (29' by 1' 3", in which the viewer may perhaps come close to making out something not unlike a hamadryad "in crim. con." with a giant praying mantis, although Lancelot Costive is by no means convinced, as if it really made any difference in the first place!); "Art Department: 1965" (live railroad torpedoes cunningly concealed in the paint are in some remote sense the *clef* to this magisterial late Cohen).

This truly amazing "show" will be on view until April 14th. The artist has kindly consented to be present in Deering (clad in his Zen robes) every afternoon from 2 to 5:45 to answer questions; he will also from time to time rap out snappy little rhythms on his Tibetan clack-dish. Tea and *petits gateaux* will be served whenever possible in the circumstances by ladies from the University Guild under the supervision of Mrs Constance Cohen. Visitors are urged to deposit used chewing-gum in a receptacle specially marked for that purpose!

1965

ET IN ARCADIA EGO?

Erminia and the Shepherd

NORTHWESTERN UNIVERSITY ARTFELLOWS
Artfellows Hall   Evanston, Illinois

Dear member:

Your officers in the NU ARTFELLOWS are happy to be able to present you — as a special bonus — with the enclosed engraving of "Erminia and the Shepherd(s)," a famous episode in Torquato Tasso's epic poem, *Jerusalem Delivered.* This handsome engraving is attributed to Filippo Aldirisio (1500-1599), who was affectionately known to his contemporaries as "Il Puzzone," as he continues to be to art historians. The engraving was most certainly made by the artist himself from his painting of the same subject which has for several centuries been the pride of the Museo Civico of Monteputtana, in the Italian heel ("an Italian heel town," as critic Carlo Conditto once wittily phrased it).

The following account of the painting (and hence of the engraving) is from a long essay by Professor M. I. T. Grant which appeared for the first time in *The Burlington Magazine,* special supplement *hors série,* Autumn, 1937.

Il Puzzone's noble version of this ever-popular episode is clearly the work of his vigorous middle years, before he became afflicted with that trembling which is reflected — though with no loss of genius! — in the paintings of his hardly-less-vigorous old age. In this striking painting of the pre-proto-baroque, the beautiful Erminia passes swiftly across a peaceful Arcadian landscape in the company of the friendly old shepherd, Rocco, who seems to be offering her the skirt which she has perhaps mislaid; two of his sheep loyally gambol in keeping with their master's joyous mood. Erminia's splendid helmet has just flown off her head (upper right) in the very exuberance of the moment! But the spirit of sleepy Arcadia softly breathes in the figures at lower right — simple barnyard creatures, evidently: a sort of pig, a duck or pouter pigeon, a mongoose. To the left of them a skull reminds us where we are and where *it* is! In the upper left corner (to complete the powerful diagonal with attenuated S-curve so typical of the late pre-proto-baroque which runs from the pig's rump through Erminia's handsome legs and old Rocco's ear) a small cherub sails blissfully by, apparently oblivious of the happenings in the busy world of shepherds and lady-warriors. In the background the painter has included glimpses of Mounts Fujiyama (left) and Popocatépetl (center), as well as the Bernese Oberland bathed in the soft light of an early Spring morning. "Beata solitudo — sola beatitudo" — how quickly these words spring to the mind as we contemplate Il Puzzone's vision — one of many, to be sure, and how different from the one in Minneapolis! — of the Arcadian ideal as caught by Tasso and himself.

We are delighted to be able to share with you the precious small collection of these engravings, unique in the world, which has quite recently come into our possession.

Fraternally yours,

"Ed" Vasari
Corresponding Secretary, NUAF

P. S. Our Treasurer informs me that on checking his records he finds you ——————————— behind in your payment of dues. To put *his* mind at rest, won't you please rectify this oversight?

1966

The Problem of Time

(The theory, held by some students—Bernard Mosher, for example—that Shakespeare's copious genius was probably rewarded at the Elizabethan equivalent of a nickel a word, may seem in part borne out by the following passage from *Henry VII,* Act I, scene 3. It is of course Shakespeare heard on the stage that lends weight to this theory. The numerous rhymes suggest an early work. What characters named Cassino and Alfonso are doing in a play named *Henry VII* has never been satisfactorily explained, and the suggestion of W. W. Douglas that Shakespeare "was having his public on" seems rather contemptible.)

CASSINO: Canst thou tell me the time of day, my lord?

ALFONSO: Aye, that I can and may and shall, perchance,
And could and would and might and mayhap should,
And likely will, though nought compels me to't,
Now that the sun his fever'd race hath cours'd
Into the west and left the east all dark,
Dim and obscure, as when there is no light
To make things plain and therefore visible,
But all the world turns blacker than the maw
Of some dread Stygian monster which doth gulp
His trembling prey that hath lost heart to live—
Yet now meseems the thread of my discourse
Is strangely tangled and its end quite hid,
Its meaning and its purport hard to see—
What *was* the question, friend, thou putst to me?

CASSINO: I asked, my lord, if thou didst know the hour?

ALFONSO: Why didst thou not more plainly, then, good sir,
Hang up thy query on this biting air
Which winter with his furious blasts hath brought
To chase the rage of summer out of thought?
But what *is* time, if *thou* canst ask it thus?
'Tis here, 'tis there, 'tis minus, and 'tis plus!

CASSINO: I know not, sir, what these thy words denote.
A simple man, unlearn'd, I did but pray
If thou couldst let me know the time of day...

ALFONSO: Give heed, then, friend; lend me thine eager ear—
Incontinent shalt thou the true time hear:

142

Though more than seven it is less than eight
And now the long hand runs at such a rate
That he offends the nose of lowly six,
Yet lingers not, but ever onward ticks.

CASSINO: Most gracious lord, my humble thanks receive,
For now I may in peace of mind take leave;
I'll beg for thee and thine the grace of heav'n,—
Bless thee who tellst me it is half-past seven!

1966

Letter for a Festschrift

Many respected Professeur Apple [sic,] [1]

22 Mai 1969

Your lettre addressed since many month to New Wye finally catch me here in hôpital of Caurina wher I am lieng cloué au lit on acont fractturd ankle now hangd in traction, thus helploss. I in large rom with three more individus which allday bavardent about nothings, allnihgt makes loud snors, spitings, éructations, borborygmes, allso two postes of télévision and courants d'air.[2] Un vrai supplice and I do not evn to mention the food! Stil is my heart strong in spite what my "friend" writs about it,[3] it bumps[4] finely I am thanking you!

Pleas to for giv my writtng is not eassy in flat up on back position allso to excuse my old fontaine pen stylo which may be making som splodges,[5] pleas allso for giv my english which I have learn now manny years but writ onely few usuely with helpfull aidings of good friends, I much preffer to writting you in french or mostly in Russian, and if I print I hope to be so in our beautifull *kirillitsa*[6] so méprisé by my "friend" le translitérateur! But I

Editor's note: The above communication was written on stationery of CAU-RINA UNIVERSITY: *Department of Slavic and Baltic*. On the first sheet these names are loosely canceled, and the words "Caurina General Hôpital [*sic*]" inserted in the same hand as that of the text of the letter. This letter has been transcribed, and arranged for the press, with notes, by editorial associate W. B. Scott.

1. This will be the last *sic* in these notes. Professor P.'s letter is printed here as closely as possible as it left his pen. His control of English spelling and idiom, remarkable in one so profoundly non-Anglo-Saxon, seems nonetheless at moments a bit uncertain—but there is no need to drown him in a flood of condescending *sics*! As for the handwriting, it hovers with passionate intensity (as one might almost say) between an unqualified Russian script for the occasional Russian word or phrase, and a sort of qualified Russian script for the English and occasional French. The transcriber—no expert at this sort of thing!—has done his best.

2. For Professor P.'s feelings about noises and drafts, see *Pnin, passim*.

3. For Professor P.'s heart, see *Pnin, passim*.

4. pumps [?] The handwriting is unclear.

5. splotches [?] Could Professor P. have been aware that "splodges" is in fact an acceptable alternative form?

6. The Cyrillic alphabet (in Russian script in the original). For V.N.'s animadversions on this alphabet, see his Commentary on *Eugene Onegin*, III.398-9.n., and—more recently—*Ada*, 84. For his transliterations of Russian, see his English works, *passim*.

144

most not risk to doeng so!

Now I most explan that I am sevrl year retiret, this year 1969 on 3 février julians calendrier I have become seventy one years aged. So since som years I retired from New Wye with great farwel banquet, even much locall native *shipuchnoe vino*[7] allso kind speches and songs, allso gift of expensive real lether valise en veau silver innitials! *Et voilà pour mon "friend" and all his labels.*[8] Since my retraite I am more busyer as ever, ghest lectureur to manny universités, importants savants which invit me, state university Bufalo on kind invitation Prof. Milton Shakespeare,[9] Grand Tetons Universitey, Aardvaark wher verry distinguish Professeur Barry Vélin[10] holding Cosa Nostra chair in manny langages invit to me, université California at Tehachapi,[11] Hayford Institute,[12] and actuely this term Caurina University wher last Friday I have sliped from low plateforme and casser ankle while makeng conférence on death of Ivan Ilyich. I am then caryd to this excelent but nosy[13] hopital in police voiture ambulance with

---

7. sparkling wine, "bubbly" (in Russian script in the original).

8. libels [?] See *Pale Fire,* 112, 163, 189, 200 (Lancer Books paperback). The sentence is heavily underlined in the original.

9. Professor Milton Shakespeare is Director of Advanced Sophomore Literary Hermeneutics at the New York State University at Buffalo, and a frequent contributor to *The New York Review of Books.*

10. Professor Barry Vélin is Chairman of the Department of Omniliterature at Aardvaark (amusingly, an "Aardvaark" figures fleetingly in *Ada!*), and the author of numerous books and articles, which range from *Old Sardines* (a small volume of whimsical aphorisms) to the by-now-classic omniliterary study, *The Confident Smirk in World Literature from Homer to Lo Hung Dong* (xlviii + 698 pages, New York and Calcutta, 1954; also paperback in Petarade Books, Chicago). (Lo Hung Dong, b. 1923, the Taiwanese *feuilletoniste,* has been described by Andalusian sinologist Alfredo Graff y Ananas as "blending in his subtle *chung* [Chinese] fashion a whisper of Kafka with a soft footfall of Borges, to venture for the moment only the most obligatory names.")

11. The Tehachapi "branch" of the University of California is powerful in Russian and Bulgarian under the forceful chairmanship of Mexican slavophile Andrés del Campo y Chapucerias.

12. The Department of Languages and Literatures at the Hayford Institute of Human Engineering is headed by Dr. Bernard Mosher, whose *Zénaïde Fleuriot et le monde slave* (Toulouse, 1946) remains pre-eminent in its field. Professor P. lectured at Hayford in the autumn of 1967 on the writings of Prince Sergei Shirinsky-Shihmatov (1783-1837).

13. noisy [?] Again the handwriting is unclear.

145

loud sirin scremming, allso flashy lihgt I am told by some students.

Now you are askng in lettre to me if I mihgt contribuer to in honneur of my old "friend" numéro? Why shold I, sir? may I francly to demand? Yes of corse I know him since many years but not as he is fond to pretendng.[14] Francly is he tryng to run[15] my life as manny peuples well know this, he has bassed his pretendue narration on manny inventions *(vïdumki)*[16] allso on cruel mimicrys by amateur cabotins like late Cockrel,[17] who I am informmed has been strick[18] by fatale crise cardiaque whil makenng one mor *verry funy*[19] imitation, but this time *was not of myself, was of my "friend" self!!*[20] Ha! Ha![21] C'est bien fait pour M. Cokrel!!

Evvery wher are ennemis, upping eybrous when is mention my name. Onely to say this name is enohg then the eybrous and manny little small smiles, allso clins d'oeil. And who is the faute? You most know ther is onely but one single onswer! So why most I writ for your revue Tri quortrley about this "friend" be cause evvry wher are allso *true* friends who say rihgt my name with out smilling or to sneze or *"prepostrous little explosion."*[22]

So you know it is verity, sir, some tims in America on manny campuss I am oftn by folish peuples beng evn mistackn to be this "friend"?! Then truely am I feling like shodowe of a shade when these are sayng, O ho, you are un tel, mentiong his name, of corse then soon they allways posing same questions about that

---

14. See *Pnin*, 185 (Atheneum paperback edition).

15. ruin [?] Either word would seem to fit.

16. So in the original—the English word followed by its Russian equivalent in Russian script and in parentheses.

17. For the late Professor John Cockerell's elaborate imitations of Professor P., see *Pnin*, 36 and (especially) 187-89.

18. stricken [?] struck [?]

19. Heavily underlined in the original.

20. Heavily underlined in the original.

21. "Ha! Ha!" inserted above the line, perhaps as an afterthought. (In Russian script in the original: "Xa! Xa!")

22. In quotation marks and heavily underlined in the original. See *Pnin*, 32.

best saling yong "lady" with spainisch name, or why love I not Dostoevsky?!! Stendhal?! Fomann? [Thomas Mann?] or how is to be cald buterflie just flitring by in air,[23] or why is my fond interst of squrls?[24]

Une heure latter, pleas to for giv. Now have I terminatd lunch, vegtebal soupe, som things like macaroni and ches, *drozashchee zhelyonoe zhelo*[25] salade, a piece spices cake too drie, allso wek tea. One television poste now has bassbal other a senator the sound of senator seems comeng from bassbal the sound of bassball from senator, my rom compagnons I can hear chatring a about bassbal, allso a bout chirurgicale interventions, gas, *o kateterah, kishkah.*[26] In to my memoiry sudenly comes poet Yuvenal, *zdorovïi duh v zdorovom tyelye.*[27]

No, esteamd Professeur Apple I can not see what I can truely writ about my "friend" of who the Russian books I can not finnish them or his english understand! Avant-hier while I *dremal*[28] malgré l'éternelle television and rum compagnon nose [29] som boddy has leaved to me the book Ada, I do not know may be some collègue from department Slavic and baltic Caurina université wher I am actuel visstng Emeritus professeur. Who cold be doing? Of corse even if this *uzhasno tyazholaya kniga*[30] mihgt be in Russian I can not be reding it whil flat up on back leg suspendue in air! I have heared it is beng about the inceste well sir if inceste I need I can allwayes go back to Sofokles allso Ovide! Who is neding more of inceste? Not I to be sure! In Sofokles is the best! So manny terrble bookes now to day! This Ada, then

---

23. For some thoughts on butterflies, see *Pnin*, 128.

24. squirrels [?] girls [?] The handwriting is decidedly unclear at this point, and a bad "splodge" compounds the difficulty. In *Pnin* squirrels are more important than girls, while in other works of this author the reverse appears to be true.

25. trembling green Jello (in Russian script in the original).

26. about catheters, bowels (in Russian script in the original).

27. Juvenal's famous "mens sana in corpore sano" (*Satires* X, 356). (In Russian script in the original.)

28. was dozing (in Russian script in the original).

29. room companions' noise [?] The handwriting again! See above, notes 1 and 13.

30. terribly heavy book (in Russian script in the original).

terrible *portnoi*[31] I hear of, allso Fruits of the M L A I am told by student to who I demand what is mening of this name but I have attendet to manny conventions of M L A and is not true! No, M L A is filld of veritabel genuin men![32] Allso feuilletant this book Ada I can see it make manny jokes about prety Chateaubriand poem[33] wich I have learn as skolboy, allso making fune and jokes with manny other not onely my "friend's" usuel joks such as Fyodor Mikhailovich Dostoevsky no doute but allso Lev Nikolaiovich Tolstoi, Sergei Timofeievich Aksakov,[34] beatifull Bérénice of Racine[35] Dr. Mertvago[36] *i pr. i proch.*[37]

No! Dear Sir I find that I can not writ nothing for your especial numéro! Too many memoirys, sir! insults, trahison! Now most I think actuely onely about my own travaux of manny years son to be complett if it suffices the time and force.[38] Now

---

31. In Russian script in the original. In Russian *portnoi* means "tailor," a fact of some symbolic significance in a recent novel whose hero is forever taking his pants off, according to critic Norman Empson, in *Gag,* June-July 1969.

32. A vigorously loyal yet strangely cryptic statement! Attempting to reconstruct its background one imagines some lightminded student "introducing" innocent Professor P. to arcane American idiom and informing him in "far out" "deadpan" labored jest that Edmund Wilson's *The Fruits of the M.L.A.* (1969) is an account of sexual deviation in the Modern Language Association, rather than the collection of small devotional exercises which it is in fact.

33. The "romance," *Le Montagnard Emigré,* sung by the French prisoner of war in Granada in Chateaubriand's story, *Les Aventures du dernier Abencerage,* figures importantly—variously altered!—throughout *Ada:* see for example 138-39, 141, 233, 241, 428, 530.

34. 1791-1859, author of such works as *A Family Chronicle* (1856) and *Years of Childhood* (1858). In an admiring account of him in *A History of Russian Literature,* 288, Prince D. S. Mirsky links Aksakov with time and Proust—"only [Aksakov] was as sane and normal as Proust was perverse and morbid, and instead of the close and stuffy atmosphere of the never aired flat of the Boulevard Haussmann there breathes in Aksakov's books the air of the open steppe." On the other hand, the translator of *Eugene Onegin* in his Commentary (III.139) describes Aksakov as "a very minor writer, tremendously puffed up by Slavophile groups . . ." An Andrey Andreevich Aksakov is a very minor character in *Ada.*

35. See *Ada*, 231.

36. This family name figures lightly (although a matter of life and death) in *Ada or Ardor: A Family Chronicle* and even more lightly in S. T. Aksakov's *Semyeinaya Hronika (A Family Chronicle*—see above, note 34). Consult the author's (Aksakov's) interesting footnote on the name (8th edition, Moskva, 1895, 146).

37. And much much more (in Russian script in the original).

38. For Professor P.'s great work, see *Pnin*, 39.

must I stop to writ my arm is tird and I have swetty itch bitwen omoplates but of corse no norse com to my lihgtng!³⁹ To morowe visttng hour will I speack to my admirable étudiante Varvara Ivanovna H. about this book Ada whch I am sur she has read it no doute! It is great déception to me that she much admire works of my "friend" both Russian and in english, but allways am I tryng showng to her true beautés of *veritable great Russian litterature!*⁴⁰ *O Rus'!*⁴¹ But dear yong Varvara Ivanovna at least knowes who am I realy in fact personely, *not*⁴² by *"friendily"*⁴³ calomnies!

Now most I to achieve my lettre dearly most estemd Sir, manny good wish to you and I thank you, I am your most respectfuley faithfull serviteur, and with fervant handshak,

> TIMOFEY PAVLOVICH PNIN [*signed*] Professor Emeritus (being corrently ocupyd with manny *great*⁴⁴ Russian writters, lecturng in Caurina université distinguished Visstng Emeritus Professeur)

1970

---

39 . . . . of course no nurse comes when I turn on my light [?]
40. Heavily underlined in the original.
41. In Russian script in the original. A famous pun, in this context rich in overtones: Horace's *O rus!* (O country-home, *Satires,* II, vi, 60) and *Rus',* the old form of *Rossiya* = Russia. For a note on Pushkin's use of this wordplay as the motto to Chapter Two of *Onegin,* see the Commentary, II.217.
42. Heavily underlined in the original.
43. Heavily underlined in the original.
44. Heavily underlined in the original.

A "Bob" Brown Sampler:
Morceaux choisis from the Novels by "Herb" Johnson

Note: *In response to persistent demands* TriQuarterly *has commissioned staff researchers W. B. Scott and Gerald Graff to bring its readers selections from the "Bob" Brown novels of "Herb" Johnson, works very much on the skirmish-line of contemporary fiction. These selections follow brief biographical and critical introductions to "Herb" Johnson and his* oeuvre; *in addition there are, between excerpts and in square brackets, materials designed "hopefully" to aid the reader: fragments of critical notices, statements by "Herb" Johnson anent his intentions, and exchanges between the researchers themselves.*

A note on the author

> "Teach him how to live,
> And, oh! still harder lesson! how to die."
> —*Bielby Porteus (1731-1808)*

"Herb" Johnson was born in Moline, Illinois, on June 16, 1930, the son of Leroy and Velma Finch Johnson. Christened Herbert Finch Johnson, he received his early education in the public schools of Moline, where he graduated third in his high school class a week before his seventeenth birthday, in early June, 1947. He entered Harvard University that fall on a Kiwanis Club

150

scholarship, planning to major in either Old Spanish or micro-biology.

At Cambridge the quiet and studious Moline schoolboy soon turned into a drunk and a public brawler, well known to town and campus police, as well as a Harvard Square "tail hound" of epic proportions. Expelled in the early Spring of his freshman year, he immediately signed on as deck hand aboard an old tanker listing heavily under a load of sheep dip for Australia. Disillusioned within minutes of putting out to sea from Boston Harbor, "Herb" Johnson has often said that his chief activities on what should have been a glamorous voyage of discovery (of himself as well as of the world) involved hours of painfully chipping rust from rust ("It was rust all the way through!"), "holding my nose," and fighting off rats, bedbugs, cockroaches, chronic headcolds and diarrhea, and the lustful advances of various weatherbeaten old shipmates armed with brass knuckles and belaying pins.

"I jumped ship at Port Said," he recounts in "Herb" Johnson Says, "and for the next eight months or so kept going at a great variety of jobs, most of which I would rather not think about today. Among other things, I was shill for a sidewalk card shark, who conned the chumps with three-card monte, the old army game; vodka distiller and distributor (a Chinese friend and I made the stuff in a dreadful little garret room); assistant to an insane Lebanese masquerading as a Hindu snake-charmer (my job was defanging the cobras, which I'm proud to remember as a job well done!); pimp and handyman for Madame Sonya Fong, an aged Eurasian full of evil who ran a string of fancy brothels which paid me off mostly in trade; prelim boy on a few fixed fight cards—I was always clever with my dukes, but in those days in Port Said if you were smart you forgot the Marquess of Queensberry rules in a hurry! Eugene O'Neill should have had it so tough!"

In May, 1949, "Herb" Johnson returned to the United States via Alexandria, Tel Aviv, Istanbul, Athens, Rome, Capri, Marseille, Paris, Lisbon, Estoril, and London, as private secretary

151

to the noted old-time film star, Wanda Kittredge, whom he had rescued from a serious beating, certain mutilation, and probable murder during an altercation in Port Said's famed "Chuck-a-luck Bar." "Keeping up with Wanda was tougher in all kinds of ways than working for Madame Fong in Port Said," he writes. "But it sure gave me a chance to see a bit more of the world and to learn the many kinds and conditions of men. Wanda and I lived only in the best hotels, high off the hog, on the cuff mostly, but what the hell . . .! She was a grand old bag, take her for all in all, with a heart loaded with larceny, and she taught me a few tricks even Port Said had never heard of!"

The outbreak of the Korean War in 1950 saw "Herb" Johnson rally loyally to the colors, "though it meant finally breaking off with Wanda—something had to give!" Sent into combat at his own request, he soon became legendary for his daring exploits as a scout behind enemy lines. Captured several times by both North Koreans and Chinese, and subjected to indescribably ingenious and excruciating tortures and various degrading humiliations in vain efforts to make him talk, "Herb" Johnson managed to escape on every occasion and return to his own lines with priceless information, his collaboration in vodka-distilling with his Port Said Chinese friend having given him an enviable command of basic Mandarin.

Armed with a medical discharge and a permanent slight hoarseness, the result of a bayonet wound, he returned to the United States in 1952 determined to make something of himself in civilian life, "even if it meant returning to Harvard." But he soon fell into a familiar restless routine which took him ceaselessly from coast to coast and border to border, as croupier in Las Vegas, Arizona real estate pitchman, "pearl diver" in a classy Chicago restaurant, gigolo at Hobe Sound during the season, fake wrestling promoter, hot-walker at Hollywood Park, karate instructor ("I knew nothing of karate but my students knew less!"), graduate student in English (on forged credentials—"It was a breeze!"), carnival roustabout, television quizmaster, lifeguard, evangelist, rivets-catcher—the list goes on and on.

A knife flashing in the hand of an enraged (and outraged) hus-
band who had returned unexpectedly to a Rogers Park (Chicago)
apartment almost brought to a bloody end the career of "Herb"
Johnson.

"But I pulled through," he writes simply yet with deep
feeling at the end of his memoir, "Herb" Johnson Says. "The
vicissitudes of life had left me permanently hoarse, with a missing
left pinkie, a ragged right ear, and only one ball. But I pulled
through—I always pulled through! Maybe somebody up there
was on my side all along. In any case, I think it beyond question
that all I had done and been, up to the very moment of first
putting pen to paper, was merely preparation for the writing of
'Bob' Brown!"

Who can say more?

W. B. S.

A critical note

> "In common things that round
> us lie some hidden truths. . . ."
> —*William Wordsworth (1770-1850)*

On the linguistic level [Raymond] Roussel answers the
requirements of criticism no better. Many have already
pointed this out, and of course negatively: Raymond
Roussel writes badly. His style is lusterless, neutral. When he
abandons the order of observation—that is, of avowed
platitude: the realm of "there is" and "is located at a
certain distance"—he always employs a banal image, a hack-
neyed metaphor, itself the standby of some arsenal of literary conventions. Lastly the auditory organization of the
sentences, the rhythm of the words, their music does not
seem to raise any problem for the author's ear. The result is
almost continuously without attraction from the point of
view of belles-lettres. . . . Thus we are dealing with the exact
opposite of what is conventionally called a good writer:

153

Raymond Roussel has nothing to say, and says it badly. . . . And yet his *oeuvre* is beginning to be acknowledged as one of the most important in French literature in the early part of this century, one which has exercised its spell over several generations of writers and artists, one which we must count among the direct ancestors of the modern novel; whence the continually growing interest that attaches today to his opaque and disappointing works.

Let us consider first the opacity. It is, quite as much, an excessive transparency. Since there is never anything beyond the thing described, that is, since no supernature is hidden in it, no symbolism (or else a symbolism immediately proclaimed, explained, destroyed), the eye is forced to rest on the very surface of things. . . . What we get, then, is an opacity without mystery: as behind a painted back cloth, there is nothing behind these surfaces, no inside, no secret, no hidden motive.

In this fashion Alain Robbe-Grillet describes the nouveau roman *technique of Raymond Roussel, a technique which he has employed in his own fiction and which bears superficial resemblance in many respects to that employed by "Herb" Johnson, author of the "Bob" Brown novels. But to classify "Herb" Johnson as a mere "new novelist," in the currently fashionable sense, is to ignore the enormous difference between the timid, stumbling, inchoate, and half-realized gropings of such precursors as Roussel, Robbe-Grillet, and Beckett, and the truly-revolutionary originality of "Bob" Brown. . . .*

To point out that "nothing ever happens in a 'Bob' Brown novel," as well-meaning critics are wont to remind us, is too often to assume that the events which do not happen to "Bob" Brown are of like kind, character, and import with the events which do not happen in so-called new novels. . . But closer scrutiny reveals that there is a world of difference between the actually rich anti-*meaning of the new novelists ("life is meaningless," "life is boring," etc.) and the wholly bland and innocuous*

154

non-*meaning of "Herb" Johnson. Thus, with respect to the presentation of character, one of the distinguishing marks of the primitive new novel is the strained attempt to avoid psychology or "character analysis" or anything which suggests there is something beneath the surface of human choice and action. By contrast, "Herb" Johnson achieves much the same effect, but more naturally, without succumbing to any such fetish of avoidance. "Bob" Brown's innermost thoughts, even at one point his dreams, are copiously particularized throughout the "Bob" Brown novels, yet with scarcely any disturbance of the tone of boneless evenness which governs the whole...*

G. G.

morceaux choisis

"And common is the commonplace
And vacant chaff well meant for grain."
Alfred Lord Tennyson (1809-92)

1

... At roughly about 10:35 or 10:40 on the morning of a Tuesday or Wednesday in May (June?) "Bob" Brown tried to recall some of the things that had happened during his second year at State Normal Tech, but was unable to. He picked up a piece of paper for a second, then put it down, looked at but did not focus on a spot on his sleeve, then lit one of his nine remaining cigarettes—in the pack in his pocket, that is, as he had two full new cartons in his bottom dresser drawer—and puffed. THE END

from "Bob" Brown's Second
Year at State Normal Tech

[from the reviews: *"Readers who followed 'Bob' Brown through his first year as English and Speech instructor at State Normal Tech may now follow him through his second year in* 'Bob' Brown's Second Year at State Normal Tech, *in which author*

155

'Herb' Johnson repeats many of the characters and incidents of the earlier work in his familiar style."

Bernard Mosher in *The Tuckpointer,*
October 8, 1962

"I tried to do pretty much the same thing all over again in 'Bob' Brown's Second Year at State Normal Tech *as I did in* 'Bob' Brown's First Year at State Normal Tech."

author "Herb" Johnson
in an interview with
interviewer "Fred" Jones.]

2

Early on a June afternoon towards the end of his third year at State Normal Tech "Bob" Brown thought idly of the summer vacation which lay ahead—the usual three months of dozing and drowsing in the large family "cabin" at Hayford's Landing on Lake Hayford, a resort in southeastern Kansas, with lots of catfish to eat washed down with "Dr. Pepper," and frequent conversations with his great-uncle, also named "Bob" Brown, a onetime shoe clerk. (This great-uncle was known to family and friends as "Old 'Bob' Brown" to distinguish him from the instructor in English and Speech at State Normal Tech, who was known as "Young 'Bob' Brown.")

The phone rang.

"Hello?"

"Hello. Is this Professor Brown?"

"Yes."

"This is 'Norm's Chevrolet,' Professor Brown. Your Chevy II is ready."

"Oh, thank you. I hope you didn't find anything seriously wrong with it."

"No, sir. You are going to need a new set of spark plugs sooner or later, but this time we just replaced a few minor parts that were worn out."

156

"Oh, that's good. How much will the job cost?"

"Seventeen ninety-five, inclusive of parts and labor."

"Well, that's not too bad. Thank you. I'll pick the car up later today."

"All right, professor. It will be here waiting for you. Good-bye."

"Good-bye."

As he hung up the phone "Bob" Brown glanced at his face in the mirror. There was a smudge on his nose which he wiped off with his right thumb. Another year almost over, he thought. What had happened? Well—there had been that morning in late January or early February when Miss Elyse Levine of Milwaukee had dropped one of her contact lenses, but within three minutes it had been found by Carl Kakemono, a Japanese-American boy from Kenosha—really far more American than Japanese—and the class in English B208 (The Modern American Novel) had resumed its peaceful discussion of theme and symbol in George Barr McCutcheon.

A large bluebottle fly buzzed for a moment at the open window, then flew away.

"It's lucky the screens were already in," "Bob" Brown thought.

THE END

from *"Bob" Brown's Third
Year at State Normal Tech*

[from the reviews: *"Readers of 'Herb' Johnson will find themselves very much at home in* 'Bob' Brown's Third Year at State Normal Tech. *Except for something of a 'surprise' ending this novel repeats most of the characters and incidents of the earlier books in this 'series.' "*

Bernard Mosher in *The Tuckpointer*
October 10, 1963

"I'd like to call the attention of reviewers to the fact that in 'Bob' Brown's Third Year at State Normal Tech *I was trying to*

do pretty much the same thing all over again that I had done in 'Bob' Brown's First Year at State Normal Tech *and in* 'Bob' Brown's Second Year at State Normal Tech."

author "Herb" Johnson in an
interview with interviewer
"Fred" Jones.]

3

As "Bob" Brown strolled along Washington Street towards his apartment following the pleasant though typically uneventful conversation with his department chairman, Dr. Claude Rogers (Rutgers B.S., Lehigh M.A., Northwestern Ph.D.) he was once again aware of the people and buildings so familiar to him from many walks from and to his apartment, which was near the corner of Washington and East 13th Street, five and a quarter blocks from the main gate of the campus. In front of the Lin Shan-li "Big Golden Chopsticks" Chinese-take-home-food establishment with its hanging red-and-gold sign, the proprietor, thirty-five-year-old Mr. Lin Shan-li, was deep in conversation with an elderly Chinese-American truck farmer, Mr. Wallace Mao—they were discussing, in subdued Cantonese, the current prices of soy beans, lichi nuts, and monosodium glutamate as compared with the prices of those articles a year and two years earlier.

At about the moment "Bob" Brown walked by these two "food dispensers" and fourteen blocks to the west Mr. Harold Anspacher, a Methodist layman, absent-mindedly drove his maroon 1962 Rambler sedan through the red light at the corner of 11th Street and Nelson Avenue. Immediately realizing his error he promised, speaking half aloud to himself, never to repeat it. Fortunately there were no other vehicles in or near the intersection at the time, and the only "witness" to Mr. Anspacher's transgression of the traffic code was little three-and-a-half-year-old Terry Williams, Jr., who was playing in the front yard of the attractive Williams home at 1412 West 11th Street, and who of course noticed nothing out of the way although even a child of his age might have become excited or frightened if Mr. Anspacher's momentary carelessness had resulted in a collision with another vehicle. Five or six minutes after the maroon Rambler had disappeared from view, Terry Williams' mother, Eleanor Bixby Williams, a Radcliffe dropout, called him into the house from a second-floor window.

Although "Bob" Brown could not understand or even guess at what the two Chinese gentlemen were talking about, the sight of them and of the sign in Mr. Lin Shan-li's window—TAKE HOME! DELICOUS [sic] CANTONESE DISHES—COOK [sic] TO ORDER—suggested to him that one of these days or weeks soon he must order some Chinese food, not so much because he was especially fond of it as because it would give him another chance to experiment with the ivory chopsticks which many years before a distant cousin who at that time was a deck officer on a freighter had brought back from Shanghai as a present for the then very young "Bob" Brown. For some years during his adolescence one of the chopsticks had been missing and presumed lost, but it had turned up stuck in the baseboard behind an old cupboard when his mother had the kitchen remodeled. "Bob" Brown still felt awkward with chopsticks. He had once asked for help from his friend and colleague at State Normal Tech, Dr. Irving Foo, instructor in sociology with three degrees from the University of Pennsylvania, but Irving Foo had not been able to help, for although of pure Nanking blood on both sides, he had been adopted as an orphan and brought up by a kindly Jewish family in Plainfield, New Jersey, and as a consequence was much more at home in a yarmelke, at a seder, as a member of a minyan, than with anything pertaining to the Middle Kingdom. Indeed, it was the amiable father of this family who had converted the name Foo Ah-fing into Irving Foo, a compromise, since it was reluctantly agreed that the unmistakably Oriental features of the boy would probably make the name Irving Epstein impractical if not really undesirable.

Further along Washington Street "Bob" Brown noticed that Collins' grocery was advertising a special sale on garden fresh peas

159

and lima beans, brussels sprouts, and navel oranges. At the corner of Washington and Lafayette he saw a policeman get out of a squad car to buy a newspaper from the vendor, Stanley Pollak, a friendly deaf dwarf with a cleft palate and a great eagerness to please. From him "Bob" Brown always purchased his regular afternoon paper as well as such magazines as *Newsweek, Esquire, Time,* and *Harper's.* After a fraction of a second's hesitation "Bob" Brown decided not to buy his regular copy of the paper now, but to wait until the final edition, which was usually delivered to Stanley Pollak's stand about five o'clock or a little later. Nodding to Stanley Pollak, who responded with a cheery Boobo Ber Bow [Hello, Mr. Brown] in an aureole of spittle, "Bob" Brown walked on. Just before he reached his own corner of Washington and 13th he noticed the "Didie King" diaper laundry truck pass a parked Buick station wagon in which a large black poodle lay fast asleep on the front seat. He reached the corner just as a small girl who had skipped by him a second earlier threw a chewing-gum wrapper in the gutter. A block away, down East 13th, he could see the back of the postman, Albert Finch, and the thought flashed through his mind that the mail had just been delivered.

from *"Bob" Brown's Fourth*
Year at State Normal Tech

["*... the difference between 'Herb' Johnson's stuff and, say,* Ulysses, *with its many details from the teeming Dublin of June 16, 1904, is that these details in Joyce are likely to* recur—*to become* motifs, *to acquire some sort of symbolic value. In the 'Bob' Brown books . . . this is not the case. Except for a few routine activities of 'Bob' Brown, and a few 'routine' people,* nothing is ever repeated, no one ever reappears. *So with the people and places mentioned, the momentary details, in the foregoing sample, copied at random from a 'Bob' Brown novel picked out of the shelf at random.*

"I should add here—what you as a 'Bob' Brown 'fan' must have noted on your own—that when people and 'events' (the

Morgan Av.
Nelson Av.
Smith Av.
Green Av.
Jones Av.
Martin Av.
Perkins Av.
Johnson Av.
Hughes Av.
Reynolds Av.
Washington St.
Case Av.
Kline Av.
Ames Av.
Lake Av.
State Av.
Philbrick Av.
Norton Av.

W. 16th
W. 15th
W. 14th
W. 13th
W. Lafayette
W. 11th
W. 10th
W. 9th
W. 8th
W. 7th
W. 6th
W. 5th
W. 4th
W. 3rd
W. 2nd
W. 1st

E. 16th
E. 15th
E. 14th
E. 13th
E. Lafayette St.
E. 11th
E. 10th
E. 9th
E. 8th
E. 7th
E. 6th
E. 5th

STATE NORMAL TECH CAMPUS

West Gate
North Gate
East Gate
Main Gate

Stoplight

■ Williams' Home

■ Dept. of English and Speech

"BOB" BROWN'S HOMEWARD ROUTE

■ 'Bob' Brown's Apartment

■ Stanley Pollak's Newsstand

■ Collins' Grocery

■ Big Golden Chopsticks

N

Roger Dr.

Johnson Parkway

wrong term, certainly!) are repeated, it is likely to be in exactly
the same words *every time. Thus, while we are never again likely
to see Mr. Harold Anspacher or young Terry Williams, Jr., we are
likely to re-encounter Mr. Lin Shan-li or Stanley Pollak, the
cheerful though unfortunately 'disadvantaged' news-vendor (and
in fact I believe both of them turn up hundreds of times in the
whole 'Bob' Brown series)—but always in the same words. Far
from acquiring any 'weight' or 'meaning' as a consequence of
these repetitions, such 'characters' (again the word is just no
good), or such places as Collins' grocery, seem to grow increasingly trivial (or decreasingly important). I hope this is all clear to
you."*

W. B. S. (in a note to G. G.)]

4

"Bob" Brown sorted the day's mail on the small deal table of the
mail room of the English and Speech Department of State Normal Tech, as was his custom each morning of the working day,
which, in this particular semester, happened to be Monday, Tuesday, Thursday and Friday. He found in his mail two advertise-
ments for newly published anthologies of essays to be used in
freshman composition courses, a bill from Simpson's, the local
bookstore, for six dollars and eighty-two cents, a notice from the
department secretary informing him of the proper procedure for
filing of late grade reports to the registrar, and a sheet of paper
on which there appeared four signatures below a brief mimeographed statement. ("Bob" Brown at first thought the statement
had been Xeroxed or Thermofaxed, but a second glance showed
that it had been mimeographed, probably on the department
mimeograph machine in the next room.) The four names appearing beneath the statement were "Andy" Johnson, "Bill" Perkins,
Mary Nelson, and "Ken" Martin. Of these four, "Bob" Brown
knew only two personally—Mary Nelson, a student in his two
o'clock class, and "Bill" Perkins, his colleague in the English and
Speech Department at State Normal Tech—although he knew
"Ken" Martin by sight, having once had him pointed out to him

by a friend as he, "Ken" Martin, was entering the east gate of the campus.

The mimeographed statement said: "We, the undersigned faculty and students, in view of the increasing pressures on student life today, urge the administration to extend the hours of the table-tennis room of the student union from 9:00 P.M. to 10:00 P.M. on Mondays through Thursdays and from 10:00 P.M. to 10:30 P.M. on Fridays and Saturdays."

At that moment, "Phil" Neal, another colleague of "Bob" Brown in the English and Speech Department at State Normal Tech, entered the mail room.

"Hello there, 'Bob,' " "Phil" Neal said.

"Hello, 'Phil.' "

"How are you?"

"Pretty well, thanks. And you?"

"Well, I can't complain."

"Say, 'Phil,' do you know anything about this petition on extending the hours of the table-tennis room at the student union?"

"Phil" Neal examined the sheet which "Bob" Brown handed to him, which was the piece of paper with four signatures on it which "Bob" Brown had found in his mail that morning.

"No, I don't know anything about it, 'Bob,' " he said. "First I've heard of it, in fact."

"It was in my mailbox this morning," "Bob" Brown said.

"It looks to me like a pretty reasonable idea," "Phil" Neal said. "I myself never sign petitions, though. It's just a thing I have about them, I guess."

"I put the petition in your box, 'Bob!' " It was the voice of "Bill" Perkins, who had entered the mail room unnoticed and who had overheard the conversation of "Bob" Brown and "Phil" Neal.

"Yes, some of the students asked me if I wouldn't mind circulating the petition in our department," "Bill" Perkins continued, "and I said all right. The Dean of Students has endorsed the idea and the President seems to be all in favor of it, but some of

163

the students thought it would help to get up the petition anyway, just in case."

"Well, then," "Bob" Brown said, "there doesn't seem to be any harm in signing, I should think."

"No, I can't see any," "Bill" Perkins said.

"Bob" Brown removed the "BIC" ball-point pen from his jacket-pocket and signed his name immediately below the fourth of the four signatures already on the document.

"Thanks, 'Bob,' " "Bill" Perkins said. "How about you, 'Phil'?"

"Well, I think it's a reasonable idea," "Phil" Neal replied, "but I never sign petitions. I just seem to have a thing about them, I guess."

"Suit yourself, 'Phil,' " "Bill" Perkins said. "Well, so long, fellows,"

"So long, 'Bill,' " "Bob" Brown and "Phil" Neal said.

from *"Bob" Brown's Seventh*
Year at State Normal Tech

["... *I think you'll find it just as interesting as the previous six—maybe even more so in view of the way 'Herb' Johnson has here established his 'relevance' to current problems by introducing the theme of campus protest and 'dissent!' "*

G. G. (in a note to W. B. S.)]

5

"Bob" Brown emptied the change from his trousers pockets before hanging the trousers on the back of the chair next to his bed. Then, setting the alarm of the Benrus clock-radio for eight-thirty-five A.M., "Bob" Brown turned the covers back and lay down in bed. Although it was highly unusual for "Bob" Brown to dream, tonight was an exception. "Bob" Brown dreamed he was sitting at his desk in his office in Bates Hall, the new Liberal Arts building into which the English and Speech Department at State Normal Tech had moved earlier this year, and he was correcting a batch of term papers for his sophomore class in Communications Skills. One of the papers, the paper which, in his dream, he was reading, read as follows: "Shakespeare's play, *Hamlet,* is one of the greatest plays of all time and a perennial favorite of those who have a love of literature. Many scholars have debated for many years over numerous problems in this play. Perhaps that is why it is so great. One of the most important problems in the play that I would like to discuss is motivation. . . ." At this point in "Bob" Brown's dream, "Bob" Brown's reading was interrupted by the entry of a student, "Bob" Clark, who was in waking life one of the better students in "Bob" Brown's sophomore class in Communications Skills.

"Professor Brown?" said "Bob" Clark.

"Yes," answered "Bob" Brown. "Come in, Mr. Clark,"

"Bob" Clark entered the office and sat down.

"What can I do for you?"

"Well, . . . I was just wondering, Mr. Brown, I mean, Professor Brown, . . . like, well see I've been doing some part-time work for the Junior Chamber of Commerce and we're holding a raffle on the 18th with the proceeds to go to the children of policemen injured in the line of duty. I was just wondering—that is, if you wouldn't mind—if you wouldn't mind buying a chance in the raffle."

"How much are the chances?" "Bob" Brown asked.

"Fifty cents each, sir."

"Well, in that case I suppose I can take two."

"Thanks very much, Mr.—I mean, Professor—Brown."

"Don't mention it," "Bob" Brown replied as he extracted a single dollar bill from his billfold and handed it across the desk to "Bob" Clark. "I'm sure that it's for a good cause."

"Well, I'm much obliged, sir," "Bob" Clark said, and he stood up and went to the door. Instead of leaving, however, he turned and faced "Bob" Brown. There was a brief pause.

"By the way, Professor Brown, I mean like I don't know how to say this, but I sure do enjoy what we've been doing in Communications Skills this semester. I mean, like what you've been saying about *Hamlet* and his problem of identity—I mean I really found that quite interesting."

"Well, thank you very much," "Bob" Brown said.

"Well, I've got to make an appointment at the infirmary," "Bob" Clark said. "So long, Professor Brown."

"So long," "Bob" Brown said.

It was at this point, as "Bob" Brown remembered it when he awoke the next morning, that his dream seemed to fade into indistinctness. Although "Bob" Brown may have had other dreams that evening, he had no recollection of what they were.

from *"Bob" Brown's Tenth*
Year at State Normal Tech

[from the reviews: ". . .*and the inclusion of a 'dream sequence'* in 'Bob' Brown's Tenth Year at State Normal Tech *seems to suggest. . . that 'Herb' Johnson, already noted as the boldest innovator in contemporary fiction, may be moving into yet another phase of experimental writing. . . ."*

Bernard Mosher in *The Tuck-*
pointer, October 18, 1971

"I've just been reading the latest 'Bob' Brown book, and as usual am 'bowled over' by 'Herb' Johnson's unflagging creative energy —it should be clear by now to all but the meanest intellects (names on request) that 'Herb' Johnson can do anything he chooses within the artistic limits he sets for himself, that (like the greatest artists of all ages) he has achieved total mastery *of his materials and means—so one imagines Shakespeare emitting* Antony and Cleopatra *or Proust* Le Temps Retrouvé..."

W. B. S. (in a note to G. G.)]

166

Award!

TriQuarterly takes great pride in awarding its annual Robe Grilleé Prize for the most novel novel to Herbert Finch ("Herb") Johnson, author of the "Bob" Brown books, a small sampling of which precedes. The citation reads (in part): ". . . an unflagging seeker after perfection in his chosen form, 'onlie begetter of 'le roman neutre,' 'Herb' Johnson has from the very beginning. . . ." The Prize this year is in fact several prizes in one "bag": $75,000 in tax-exempt municipal bonds; a round trip, first-class, all expenses paid, to idyllic Bali, with two glorious weeks at the Bali Hilton, for "Herb" Johnson and his girl-friend, Donna Novick; a six-pack of Wild Turkey; and an autographed photograph, suitably framed, of novelist James Jones. The awards were made at a banquet at **TriQuarterly's** rooms in University Hall, Evanston, with editor Charles ("Chuck") Newman in the chair; twenty-four jeroboams of Taittinger "Blanc de Blanc" were consumed by the guests, who represented a veritable cross-section of all that is smartest in the North Shore's world of letters. "Herb" Johnson responded to the toast by the Chairman with a few fitting words from Lucius Annaeus Seneca:

> *Perdomita tellus, tumida cesserunt freta,*
> *inferna nostros regna sensere impetus;*
> *immune caelum est, dignus Alcide labor*
> *in alta mundi spatia sublimis ferar,*
> *petatur aether . . . !*

W. 1st

W. 2nd   North Gat

West   **STATE NORMAL TECH**
Gate   **CAMPUS**
W. 3rd

East
Gate
W. 4th

W. 5th   ■ Dept. of English
                                           and Speech

W. 6th   Main Gate

W. 7th

W. 8th

W. 9th

                                                                        ■ Big G
W. 10th

W. 11th   ■ Williams' Home   ■ Coll

          Stoplight

W. Lafayette   ■

W. 13th

                                                                       ■ 'Bob'
W. 14th

W. 15th

W. 16th

"BOB" BROWN'S HOMEWARD ROUTE

Morgan Av.
Nelson Av.
Smith Av.
Green Av.
Jones Av.
Martin Av.
Perkins Av.
Johnson Av.
Hughes Av.
Reynolds Av.
Washington St.
Case Av.